American Conservatory Press

Complete Guide to Music Note Reading

by
Theodora Schulze

Copyright © 2013, American Conservatory Press, Belize, Central America

Complete Guide to Music Note Reading

by
Theodora Schulze

This sequence of programmed instruction provides a thorough explanation of every symbol of musical notation and how to execute it. It is designed for beginners with no prior knowledge of music, or for advanced players or singers who need a comprehensive review to fill gaps in their earlier training. This program was developed by the author at her private studio in the Carnegie Hall Building in New York.

This work is dedicated to the memory of the late Matilda Landsman Berg.

FOREWORD

This guide is more than a book instructing beginners how to finger the recorder. It is a complete system of study in musical notation, including a thorough explanation of every basic symbol of notation and how to execute it. Since its introduction, this instruction book has done far more than merely teach people how to hobble through familiar tunes on the recorder. In fact, the main burden of this volume is not really recorder playing at all; first and foremost, it aims to teach the interpretation and execution of musical notation. The recorder, because it is relatively easy to play in its early stages, has been chosen as a medium . . . a tool . . . a practical device on which to practice one's newly learned reading ability.

This book can be used easily in class instruction or private teaching. Its flexibility enables mixed classes, consisting of soprano and alto recorders, to learn with ease. Or, if used for mixed classes including sopranos, altos, and tenors, the tenors may play the soprano line without causing any musical dissonance. For classes consisting of sopranos only, altos only, or tenors only, the teacher plays the missing parts in the duets. In private teaching for any size of recorder, the teacher plays duets with the student.

Because of its basic nature, this method has proved highly successful both for beginners without prior knowledge of music and for advanced musicians of any instrument (including recorder) who need a comprehensive review to fill any gaps in their previous training. Holders of baccalaureate and graduate degrees from accredited musical colleges often have greater need of this material than do complete beginners. For often in our early training, the precise and comprehensive study of musical notation is passed over and great reliance placed upon "playing by ear," intuitive approximations, and other imprecise practices. Thus, a class of adult beginners may often move through these pages at a faster rate of progress and with greater ease than will a class consisting of people whose earlier exposure to musical instruction has left them with preconceived notions, bad habits, and misconceptions.

The text presented here begins with no assumption of any knowledge whatever on the part of those who approach its study. No topic is dismissed lightly; no feature of musical notation is left unexplained.

The author has had continuous success using this method for people from all walks of life and in all age brackets at her Carnegie Hall studios and elsewhere since 1954. Children from age six onward, adult beginners in music, and musicians with degrees in music have all benefited from its pages.

TO THE STUDENT

If you are a beginner in music, of course you do not know how to read musical notes. On the other hand, you may be an experienced player — perhaps even a graduate of a music school. Yet in your case also, the odds are that you have never really had a systematic and thorough training in music note reading.

Regardless of how much or how little knowledge of music you may have, this book is intended for you. Its primary objective is to teach you to read musical notation and to execute musical passages as they appear on the printed page. The recorder is treated here as a tool for that purpose.

You will soon note the complete absence of familiar tunes. The folk songs and traditional melodies which grace the pages of other instruction books will not be found here. The reason for this should be obvious: I want to be sure that whenever you play from this book, you are reading exactly what is written, not just hazarding an approximation partly from the notes and partly from memory. The habit of playing "by ear" without prior adequate grounding in music note reading is one of the most pernicious evils and is permitted — and even encouraged — by far too many teachers. It is even fancied by many teachers and parents that the ability to "play by ear" is the one and only barometer of "musical talent." Children are thus pushed into early efforts at this dangerous sport by parents and teachers who are eternally hopeful that theirs will be the next "Wunderkind."

Adult beginners, also, are often impatient to get into actual playing. In addition, they may secretly hope to discover in themselves a great talent which was denied development in their early youth by an inadequate school program or by negligent parents. So the adults also make the fatal mistake of trying to do everything "by ear."

By excluding from this book all familiar tunes, I have attempted to make certain that you will really learn to read, not half-read and half-improvise, but *really read*. Both seasoned professionals and complete beginners have benefited from earlier pilot editions of this book, and I hope you will, too.

I ask only one thing: *Do not* attempt to play any familiar music, or to play anything from memory, or "by ear", until *after* you have mastered all of the topics presented here. After that, the sky's the limit!

THEODORA SCHULZE

CONTENTS

Foreword iii
To the Student v

LESSON I

Articulation (Tonguing) 1

The Music Staff and the Treble Clef: 1
Holding the Recorder 1

Learning the First Note: *soprano*   *alto* 2
Time Values in Music (Part One):
    Beating Time; Foot-Tapping 3
Playing and Tapping 4
The Quarter Note: 4

Three New Notes: *soprano*   *alto* 5
The Double Bar-Line: 5
Conclusion:
    Note Heads and Stems: ; Breathing; Post; A Summary Exercise 7

LESSON II

Two Notes Which Introduce the Accidentals ♯ ♮ ♭: *soprano*   *alto* 8

Extending Our Range Downward: Two New Notes: *soprano*   *alto* 9
How Long Notes Are Notated and Played 10
    1. The Tie:
    2. The Half Note:
    3. The Dotted Half Note:
    4. The Whole Note:
A Summary Exercise 13

LESSON III

Two New Notes: *soprano*   *alto* 14
A Word About Bar-Lines 14
How Silence Is Notated 14
    1. The Quarter Rest:
    2. The Half Rest:
    3. The Dotted Half Rest:
    4. The Whole Rest:
A Summary Exercise 15
A New Rhythmic Concept: What Symbolizes One Beat 16
Tempo 17
Conclusion: About Lesson IV 17

LESSON IV

Seven Duets for Soprano and Alto Recorders 18

LESSON V

Time Values in Music (Part Two): Playing Half-Beat Notes 21
    1. In "Half-Note Time Signatures"
    2. In "Quarter-Note Time Signatures"
        (a) The Eighth Note: ♪
        (b) Eighth Notes in Groups; The Beam: ⊓
        (c) The Eighth Rest: 𝄾
Summary: Three Duets 23

LESSON VI

Half-Hole Technique
    Extending Our Range Upward: *soprano* ... *alto* 25
Some Remarks About Finger Position 26

Four Higher Notes: *soprano* ... *alto* 26
Two Duets 28
An Introduction to the C Major Scale 29
About Measures and Time Signatures 30
Musical Terminology: Some Further Observations 31
A Duet in 3/4 Time 31

LESSON VII

The G Major Scale (The Altos Learn F♯: ...) 32

The F Major Scale (The Sopranos Learn B♭: ...) 32

The D Major Scale (Sopranos and Altos Learn C♯: *soprano* ... *alto* ...) 32
About Keys and Key Signatures 33
    1. G Major
    2. F Major
    3. D Major
Summary: The Scales of C, G, F and D Major 34

LESSON VIII

Two New Symbols 35
    1. The Repeat Sign: 𝄇 *or* 𝄆
    2. Repeated ("Slashed") Notes
Eleven Duets, Including Music in 3/8 and 6/8 36

LESSON IX

Time Values in Music (Part Three):
    The Sixteenth Note ♪ and Rest 41
        1. Playing Sixteenth Notes: ♫, ♬♬, etc.
        2. Combinations: Sixteenth Notes and Rests; Sixteenths and Eighths
        3. Tying the Sixteenth Note
Summary: Three Duets and a Scale Exercise 43

LESSON X

Two New Notes: *soprano* ... *alto* ... 46
Three New Scales: B♭ Major, E♭ Major and A Major 46
The Chromatic Scale 46
The Naming of Note Pitches 47

LESSON XI

Time Values in Music (Part Four):
    Smaller Note Values 48
        1. The Thirty-Second Note ♪ and Rest
        2. The Sixteenth-Note Triplet:
Some Common Short-Note Patterns 49

LESSON XII

Tempo and Rhythm (Meter) 51

LESSON XIII

Three High Notes: *soprano* ... *alto* ... 55
Rhythm: Some Further Observations 55
Repetitions and Pauses 56

LESSON XIV

Learning the Last Note: *soprano* ... *alto* 57
The Slur: ⌢ or ⌣ 57
Musical Selections 58
A Summary of All Recorder Fingerings 61

Lesson I

ARTICULATION (Tonguing)

The most important single factor which will affect your future ability to play advanced music is *tonguing* or articulation. *It is most essential that this be mastered completely from the very beginning.* It is not a difficult study, but does require some diligence in the early stages.

The tongue acts as an air valve which regulates and controls all breath flow through the recorder. The tongue is held against the roof of the mouth, just in back of your front teeth, where you would customarily put it to pronounce the letter "T". Every tone which you produce on the recorder calls for the same action from the tongue as if you were pronouncing the word "toot". That is, all tones are produced not only by *beginning* with a tap of the tongue, but also by *ending* with the return of the tongue to its position of rest against the roof of your mouth to cut off the air flow through the recorder. In short, all tones are to be begun and ended with the tongue.

Often, beginning players are so intent upon mastering finger positions and new notes that they allow themselves to become careless about tonguing. They begin huffing and puffing into the instrument with no tongue action at all, leaving all matters of articulation to chance. It must be said that in so doing they tend to rob themselves of the chance to become really polished virtuoso performers later on. There should be no rush to learn fingerings. There are only twenty-seven fingerings to be learned in all, and none of them are unduly difficult. The only real problem to master on the recorder is that of tonguing clearly, and it is toward the development of good articulation that you should turn your primary attention.

THE MUSIC STAFF AND THE TREBLE CLEF

All music is written on the *music staff*, which consists of five lines arranged thus:

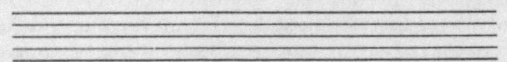

At the beginning of each line of music there appears a *clef designation*. Music for the soprano and alto recorders is written on a staff bearing a *treble clef* designation, which appears thus:

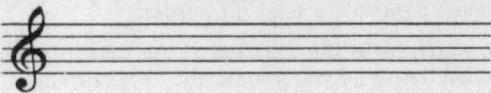

HOLDING THE RECORDER

Now, with respect to the correct method of holding your instrument, look at the following diagram:

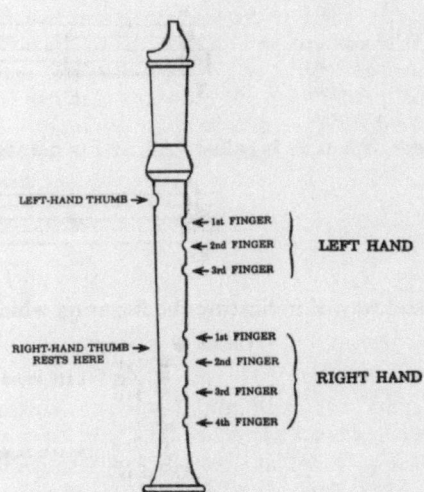

This illustration shows all the tone-holes of the recorder, and shows which fingers govern the various holes. Notice that each hole is regulated by one and only one finger, and that each finger regulates one and only one hole. The right-hand thumb rests against the back of the instrument just behind and a trifle below the first fingerhole. In that position, the thumb helps to support the instrument in the player's hands. There is no hole for the little finger of the left hand; therefore, this finger always remains idle.

The tip of the mouthpiece should be held lightly between the lips, just tight enough to maintain an airtight seal around the orifice of the windway. Neither the teeth nor the tongue should ever touch the recorder mouthpiece. It is especially important that, in tonguing notes, the tongue should never tap directly on the orifice of the windway, but should operate against the roof of the mouth (hard palate) as explained previously.

LEARNING THE FIRST NOTE:

 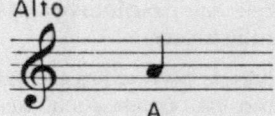

To learn the first note, proceed as follows:

Cover the thumb-hole with the left-hand thumb, and the top three fingerholes with the first three fingers of the left hand.

Place the first and second fingers of the right hand on their respective holes and leave the two remaining holes open.

Place your tongue against the roof of your mouth and then place the mouthpiece between your lips as explained above. Only about an eighth of an inch of the mouthpiece need be covered by the lips, and it is almost more correct to say that the recorder is held *up to* the lips than to say it is held *between* them.

Now, holding your fingers in place as described, gently blow into the instrument: "T-o-o-o-o-t".

There are several things to watch out for. If you have any difficulty in getting this note, then first try blowing with a softer stream of air. It is incredible to some beginners what a small breath pressure is necessary in playing on the recorder. If your first attempt to blow on the instrument produced a harsh squawk, then you must blow softer until you get a more musical tone. It is possible, on the other hand, to be too timid and not to blow a strong enough stream of air into the instrument. If your first attempt produced only a faint murmur, you must blow just a faint bit harder.

Another thing to watch for is the duration of the tones you blow. The length of time which your tones will take up depend upon how long you sustain the "vowel sound", *oo*. If you try to say *toot* just exactly as you would speak it, there will not be sufficient time between the two *t*'s to permit the emission of a musical sound. Lengthen your "vowel sound": "t-o-o-o-o-o-o-o-t".

The tone which you have just produced has a different sound on the different sizes of recorders. On the *soprano recorder*, this note is called "E", and is notated on the bottom line of the treble staff:

On the *alto recorder*, this note is called "A", and is notated in the second space of the treble staff:

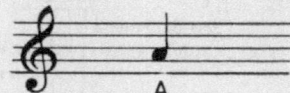

There is a shorthand way of indicating the fingering which was just used, which works as follows:

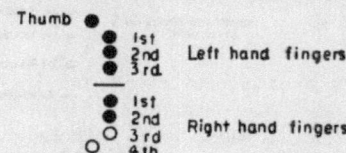

A blacked-in circle signifies a fingerhole that is to be covered, and a circle which is not blacked in signifies a fingerhole that is to be left open. This method of indicating fingerings will be used throughout our work. According to this method, the fingering just learned would be indicated as follows:

TIME VALUES IN MUSIC (Part One): Beating Time; Foot-Tapping

Before going further, we introduce the study of time relationships.

All time values in music are measured in relation to a steady series of pulses, which occur and reoccur in a regular alternation like a healthy heart beat. As a matter of fact, the pulses are called beats, after this analogy. Since the beats alternate regularly, they serve to mark off *equal intervals of time.*

Musical beats may be provided by the ticks of a metronome or other clock-type mechanism, or they may be only imagined inside the brain of the musician performing the music. The best way for beginners in music to accustom themselves to time values is to beat time on the floor with one foot. In order not to cause great commotion in doing this, a very mild type of beating should be employed — so that we say our rhythm is maintained by "foot-tapping". But it should not be forgotten that these foot-taps are, in every sense, *literally* musical beats. A musical beat is no different than any other kind of beat: it is an impact which, together with other similar impacts, serves to mark off equal intervals of time.

Let us now turn our attention to cultivating the right type of foot motion.

To begin, hold your foot so that the heel is resting on the floor and the toe is hovering about an inch and a half or so above the floor. Now let your toe fall to the floor. Let it remain there for a moment, and then lift it again to its starting position, where it should remain hovering for another moment and then be dropped to the floor again, and so on. These motions should be brisk and snappy, and should take place in regular alternation: down-up-down-up-down-up, etc.

If you have any difficulty doing this, there is a way of eradicating the difficulty. Using a mechanical clock with a fairly loud tick, time your foot motions so that there is one motion for every four ticks, thus:

<u>tick</u> - tick - <u>tick</u> - tick - <u>tick</u> - tick - <u>tick</u> - tick - <u>tick</u> - tick - <u>tick</u> - tick - <u>tick</u> - tick - <u>tick</u> - tick -
↓   ↑   ↓   ↑
down   up   down   up   *etc.*

This procedure will insure that a reasonably long time will elapse between consecutive motions. Be sure that each downward and each upward motion is brisk and snappy, and that the foot remains *motionless* in between — *motionless on the floor* from "down" until "up", and *motionless in the air* from "up" until "down". Notice also that, in the down-stroke, it is the exact moment at which the foot makes its impact against the floor which we call the *beat*. The motion of the foot *toward* the floor takes place in the instant just *preceding* the beat (impact). Similarly on the up-stroke: the upward motion of the foot takes place during the instant just *preceding* the exact moment of arrival in the "up" position. In both cases, it is the *moment of arrival* which coincides with the tick of the clock.

Now try making your foot motions twice as frequent:

<u>tick</u> - tick - <u>tick</u> - tick - <u>tick</u> - tick - <u>tick</u> - tick - <u>tick</u> - tick - <u>tick</u> -
↓   ↑   ↓   ↑   ↓   ↑
down   up   down   up   down   up   *etc.*

These exercises should serve to emphasize several things. First, the "snappiness" and "vigor" with which your foot makes its motions should have nothing to do with the length of time which elapses between successive motions. Second, when the foot snaps down, it should not snap up again instantaneously as if it had struck a hot stove. The foot should stay down, motionless on the floor, until it is time to snap up.

Once you have mastered this foot motion, keep practicing it until it becomes second nature and requires little concentration. Although the motion should be brisk and snappy, it should also be easy and relaxed. If your leg muscles tend to get cramped-feeling and stiff, you are holding them too rigid and they should be relaxed a bit.

Now begin to think to yourself as you beat (perhaps aloud at first):

```
foot motion:  down - up  -  down - up  -  down - up  -  down - up  -  down - up  -  ....
                ↓     ↑      ↓     ↑      ↓     ↑      ↓     ↑      ↓     ↑
think:        "one  -  &  -  one  -  &  -  one  -  &  -  one  -  &  -  one  -  &  -"....  etc.
                    (and)
```

"One" occurs exactly at the instant your foot strikes the floor; "&" occurs exactly at the instant your foot reaches its "up" position. Each "one" is a *beat*, and each "&" is a *subdivision* of a beat — similar in function to the half-inch marks on a ruler.

PLAYING AND TAPPING

Thus armed with a technique for counting off beats and half-beats, we are prepared to attempt regulating tones on the recorder. First, blow again the note which you have just learned ("E" on soprano, "A" on alto) so as to re-familiarize yourself with it.

Now, as you blow the note, time the "toots" so that, as your foot moves up and down, the initial "t" begins at the count of *one* and the final "t" occurs at the count of "&":

```
foot motion:  down - up  -  down - up  -  down - up  -  down - up  -  down  -  ....
                ↓     ↑      ↓     ↑      ↓     ↑      ↓     ↑      ↓
think:        one  -  &  -  one  -  &  -  one  -  &  -  one  -  &  -  one      ....
                ↓     ↑      ↓     ↑      ↓     ↑      ↓     ↑      ↓
play:         tooooot        tooooot       tooooot      toooooot      tooooo  ....  etc.
```

Keep doing this until it comes easy and seems natural.

In music-staff notation, this succession of tones is written as follows:

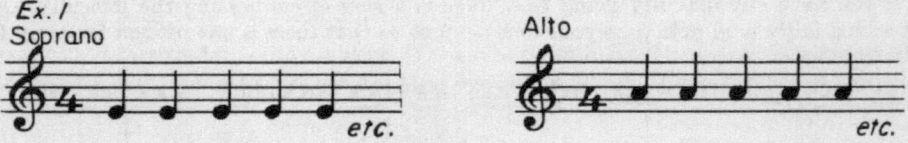

(The figure "4" placed after the treble clef is properly called a "time signature". For the time being, ignore this figure; it has no significance for us at this particular time. Its meaning will be discussed in Lesson III.)

THE QUARTER NOTE: ♩

The symbol ♩ is called a *quarter note*.

A quarter note represents a musical tone which begins on "one" and ends on "&", with a silence immediately following which lasts until the next "one".

Thus, the quarter note is composed of two equal parts, the first part being *sound* and the second part being *silence*.

We see, therefore, that a row of quarter notes stands for a series of tones alternating with silences — just as you played them a moment ago. A quarter note may appear on any line or in any space in the musical staff, but its rhythmic (i.e., *time-wise*) significance is always the same. Its position on various lines or spaces will affect only what combination of fingers you use. This should become clear as we now proceed to learn several new fingerings.

THREE NEW NOTES:

For the next fingering, cover the thumb-hole with the left-hand thumb and cover all three left-hand fingerholes. Cover the bottom fingerhole with the last finger of the right hand.

According to the shorthand notation we have adopted, the note and its fingering are as follows:

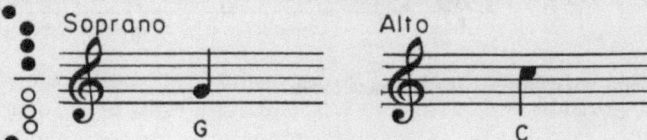

Now play the following, remembering that quarter notes are to be played as indicated in the preceding discussion:

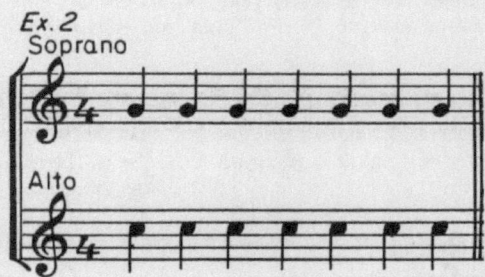

Next, play both tones in the same exercise:

THE DOUBLE BAR-LINE

The two lines drawn across the end of the staff signify the end of the exercise. The name of this symbol is the *double bar-line* (also called the "double bar"): ‖

For the next fingering, see if you can interpret it solely from the shorthand system:

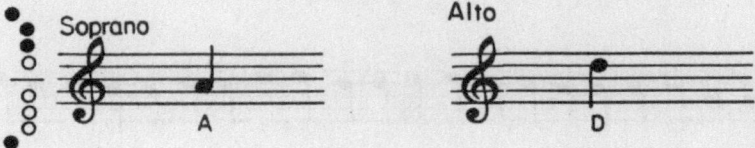

Now a quarter note exercise using this tone:

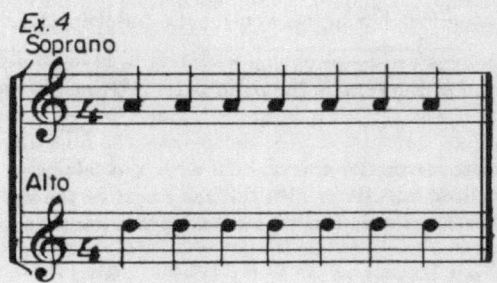

In combination with previously learned tones:

Another tone:

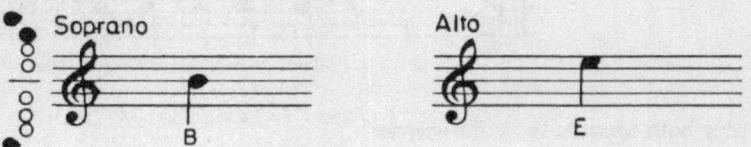

A quarter-note exercise using the new tone:

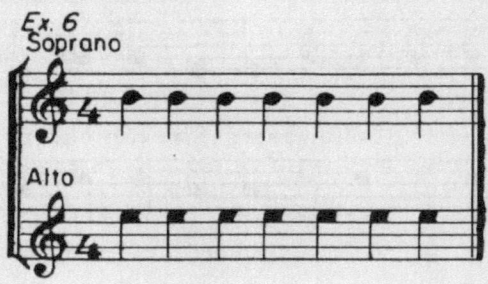

The two new tones in combination:

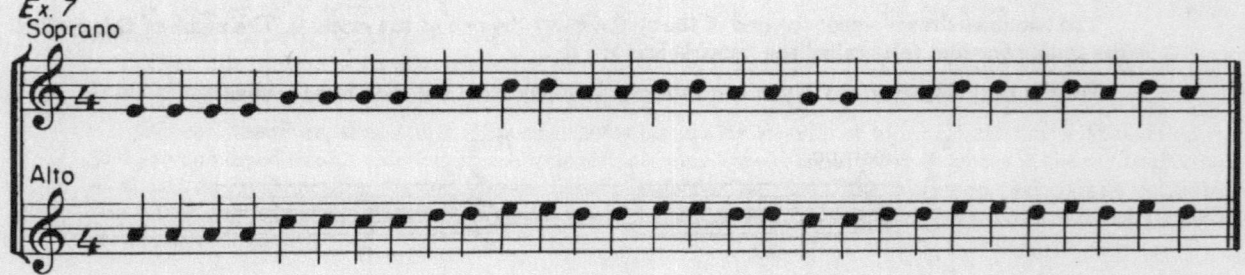

CONCLUSION: *Note Heads and Stems; Breathing; Post; A Summary Exercise*

As a conclusion to the first lesson, we append the following brief remarks:

For purposes of intelligent discussion, you will need to know that the components of a quarter note have separate names. The *head* of the note is the main part. It is, as the name implies, the solid part:

The position of the *head* on the staff is what determines the fingering to use and, therefore, the *pitch* of the note. The other component is the *stem:*

The stem has no particular importance in the case of the quarter note, but as you learn other note values in succeeding lessons you will see that the general purpose of the stem is to help make clear the rhythmic values of the notes to which it is attached.

A word on the subject of breathing: When you take a breath, be sure it is taken through the *mouth*, and never the *nose*. The nasal passages are too narrow to transmit the relatively large quantities of air involved in the process of breathing while playing the recorder.

Another thing to notice: Sometimes a quantity of stale air accumulates in the lungs, and makes you feel "short of breath". Just as the spaces between notes are utilized for taking in fresh air, so also they may be used for expelling old air. Later on, we will be playing notes which have sufficient space between them to permit both exhaling and inhaling during the same interval between notes. For the present, you will have time only for one or the other.

The "post" is customarily used as a support, in the interest of holding the recorder more steadily, for all fingerings which must be negotiated with the left hand alone. Therefore, the bottom finger of the right hand has been shown to be covered for all such fingerings. Some historical textbooks designate the ring-finger for this purpose. Either is acceptable.

The following exercise will serve as a summary of the material which we have covered:

Lesson II

TWO NOTES WHICH INTRODUCE THE ACCIDENTALS ♯ ♮ ♭ :

First, let us return to the second note or tone we studied. Do not forget to use your tongue in the correct way, both to begin and to end the tones:

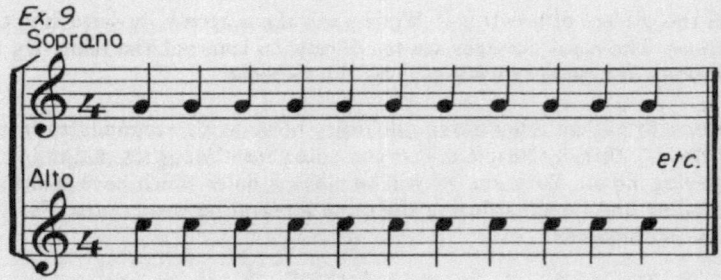

Now, a new tone:

Notice, in the soprano part, that the symbol ♯ stands for the word "sharp". Therefore, if a note has the symbol "♯" in front of it, it is called by its *letter name* plus the designation *sharp*. Thus, F♯ is called "F-sharp".

Another new tone:

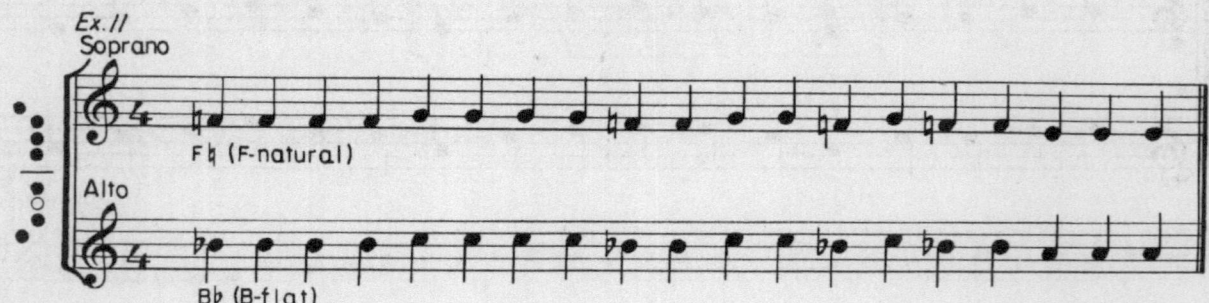

Once a ♯, ♭ or ♮ appears, it is understood that all notes on that staff line or space carrying the sign are subject to that sign unless contradicted by another, different, sign. (In this last exercise, there are nine F-naturals in the soprano line and nine B-flats in the alto line.)

The *sharp sign* (♯), the *natural sign* (♮), and the *flat sign* (♭) are called "accidentals". These accidentals may be applied to notes on any degree of the staff. If no accidental appears in front of a note, then it is understood that that note is a "natural" note, just as if the natural sign were written in front of it.

This convention serves the useful purpose of making it unnecessary to put an accidental sign in front of each of the millions of notes in printed and handwritten music. Thus, all of the notes which we covered in the first lesson were "natural" notes, since they had no accidental signs in front of them. There was no danger that anyone would play an *E-sharp* or an *E-flat*, so it was unnecessary to put a natural sign in front of the *E* when we first learned it.

In other words, the natural sign is only used in places where there might be some doubt and confusion if it were *not* used. For instance, in studying the two new fingerings just now, the soprano recorders learned *F-natural* and *F-sharp*. The natural sign had to be used in order to keep the two notes distinguished one from the other. The alto recorders learned *B-natural* and *B-flat*, and the natural sign again had to be used to avoid confusion.

In playing over these new notes, it will be noticed that when the soprano recorder plays F-natural and F-sharp, the F-sharp sounds slightly *higher* in pitch than the F-natural. Similarly, when the alto recorder plays B-flat and B-natural, the B-flat sounds slightly *lower* in pitch than the B-natural.

This is true for all notes: The "natural" note is produced by a certain fingering; the fingering prescribed for the sharp on that note will produce a tone slightly higher in pitch, and the fingering prescribed for the flat on that note will produce a tone slightly lower in pitch.

To help illustrate the foregoing remarks, review the new fingerings as given at the beginning of this chapter and then play the following exercise:

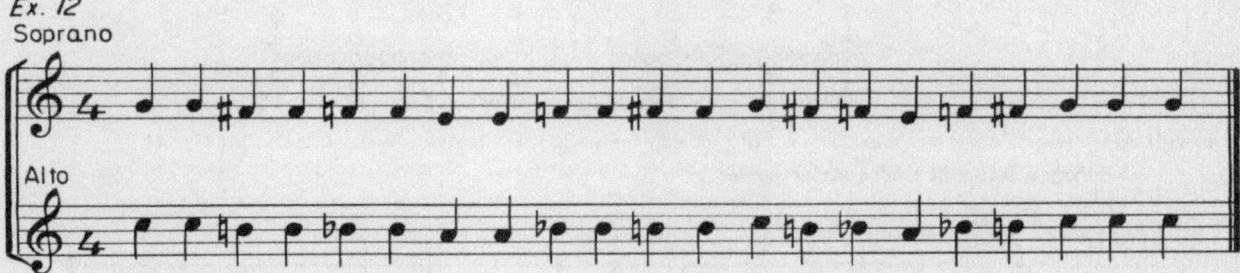

EXTENDING OUR RANGE DOWNWARD: *Two New Notes*

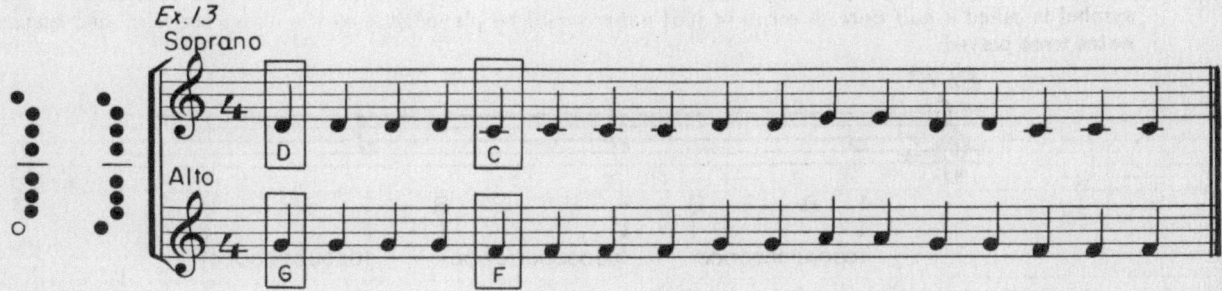

The following exercise will serve as a review of all fingerings learned so far. Be sure it is mastered well before going on.

Ex. 14

HOW LONG NOTES ARE NOTATED AND PLAYED

1. The Tie: ⌢ or ⌣

We return to the subject of rhythm, and introduce a useful symbol known as a *tie*. It looks like this: ⌢ or ⌣ , and when written over two quarter notes, it signifies that there should be a continuous sound from the beginning of the first quarter note to the end of the second quarter note.

In other words, the silence which ordinarily separates the two notes is eliminated, and *the two notes are fused together into one continuous sound*. This is illustrated as follows:

Play a series of tied quarter notes:

2. The Half Note: 𝅗𝅥

Musical sounds of this length (♩ ♩) are so numerous in musical compositions that composers have found it convenient to adopt a single symbol to represent the equivalent of two tied quarter notes: 𝅗𝅥 . This symbol is called a *half note*. A series of half notes would be played just as the above series of tied quarter notes were played:

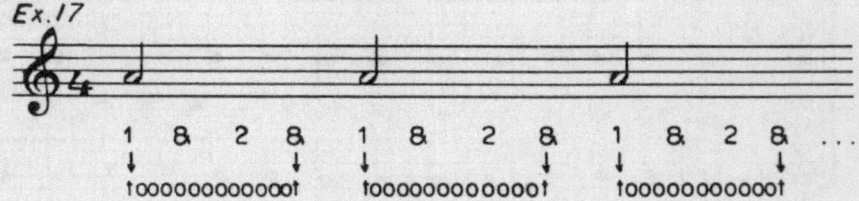

In playing a series of half notes, it is often convenient to think: "1-&-2-&-1-. .", rather than "1-&-1-&-1-. . ." thus helping the player to keep track of the number of beats involved. To get used to this new way of thinking, play the preceding exercise once again, saying to yourself "1-&-2-&-1-&-2-&-1..." Then do the same for all the half notes which appear in the following exercise.

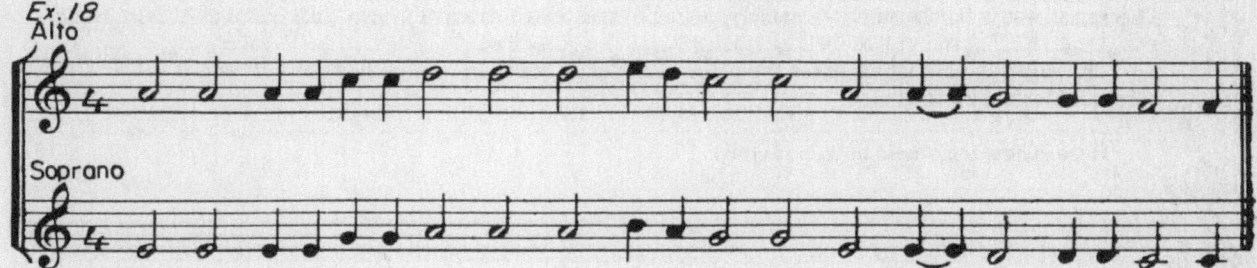

(Note that the parts were *reversed* in Ex. 18!)

3. *The Dotted Half Note:* 𝅗𝅥.

A tie may also be used to connect two notes of *different* lengths. A half note tied to a quarter note would be played thus:

Once again, there exists a single symbol which can be used to represent two tied notes — in this case, the half note tied to a quarter note. The symbol is called the *dotted half note* and looks like this:

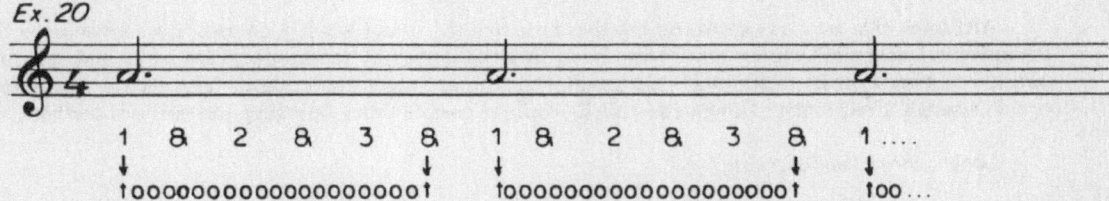

We now count to *three*, in order to help keep track of the number of beats involved.

The following exercise includes all note values learned so far:

4. The Whole Note: o

Suppose we tie together two half notes, or a dotted half note and a quarter note, or four quarter notes. The result would be the same — namely, a single tone which extends over a time interval of *four beats*.

The single symbol which takes the place of the more cumbersome methods of notation is called a *whole note*, and looks like this: o

Here is how the whole note is played:

Ex. 22

There are *four* beats involved in playing a *whole note* and there are *two* beats involved in playing a *half note*. For convenience, we say that a whole note "has" 4 beats, or "is 4 beats in length", or "is four beats long".

The half note is so named because it "has" half as many beats as a whole note.

The quarter note "has" one-fourth as many beats as a whole note, or, as we sometimes say, it is "one-fourth as long" as a whole note.

Although this way of expressing relative note lengths is not strictly correct, its convenience has led to its universal adoption among musicians. Such inconsistencies of terminology are often not adequately explained to beginners in music, with the result that the art of music tends to take on the appearance of an occult science. Frequently, things like this discourage people from pursuing the subject further.

Look now at the following:

> quarter note . . . . one beat
>
> half note . . . . two beats
>
> dotted half note . . . . three beats
>
> whole note . . . . four beats

And notice that, within the capacity of the human lungs to keep emitting a continuous stream of air, a single tone can be sustained for *any* number of beats:

Ex. 23

A SUMMARY EXERCISE

We conclude Lesson II with the following exercise:

Lesson III

TWO NEW NOTES:

We begin with two new fingerings:

A Word About Bar-Lines

You may have been disturbed by the fact that lines were drawn across the music staff at certain points in the preceding exercise. Such lines are called "bar-lines", and may occur anywhere. They should be ignored by the player for the time being since they have no significance at this stage of study. A little more will be said about bar-lines later on.

HOW SILENCE IS NOTATED

1. The Quarter Rest: 𝄽

We must now turn again to the study of rhythm and articulation. All the notes we have played have consisted of (1) a tone of some certain length, followed by (2) a silence at the end. Sometimes it is necessary to have a silence more prolonged than those which come at the end of notes, or which occupy a more prominent position than the second half of a beat. To cover these needs, we have a set of symbols called *rests*. There is a rest to correspond to each kind of note value. The *quarter rest* 𝄽 represents a silence of the duration of exactly *one beat*:

The following exercise contains some quarter rests:

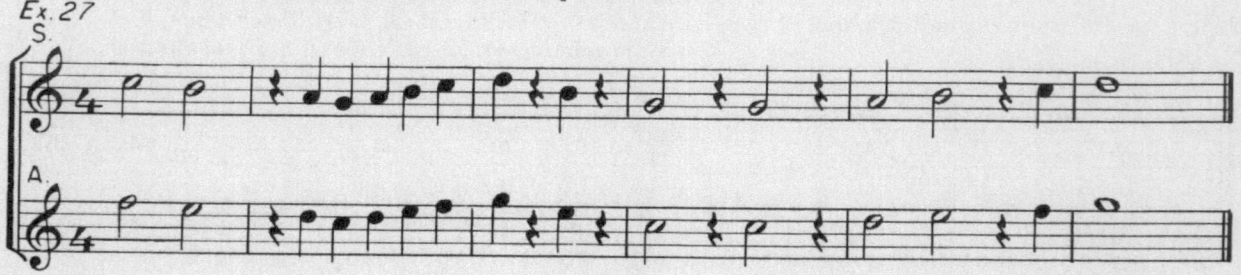

2. The Half Rest:

The *half-rest* signifies a silence of *two beats'* duration:

3. The Dotted Half Rest:

The *dotted half rest*: calls for *three beats* of silence:

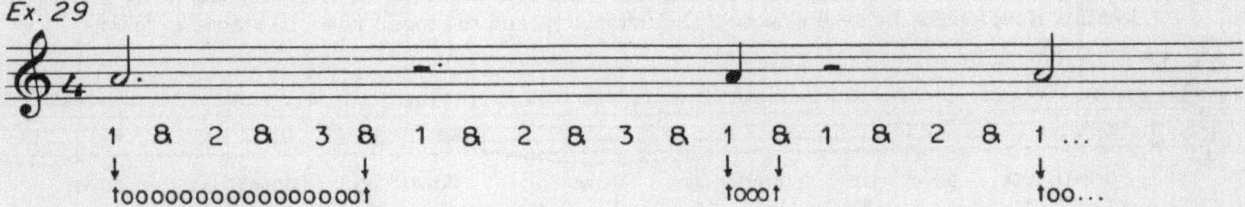

4. The Whole Rest:

The *whole rest* calls for *four beats* of silence:

A SUMMARY EXERCISE

Now a single exercise with all note values and rest values:

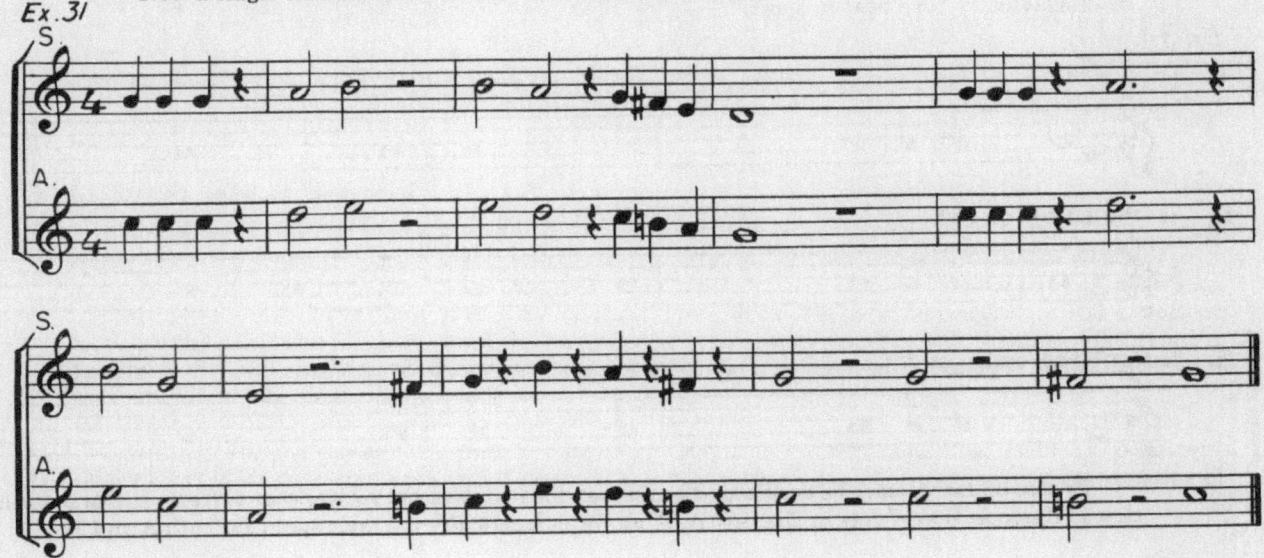

A NEW RHYTHMIC CONCEPT: What Symbolizes One Beat

Earlier, we promised an explanation of the figure "4" which appears at the beginning of all the music we have played so far. This number is of great rhythmic significance, for it tells us *what note value is to carry the value of one beat*.

Up to now the number has always been 4, which stands for the denominator of the fraction ¼. This number 4 tells the player that each time his foot goes down and up once, he has executed the rhythmic equivalent of *one quarter note*. In other words, ♩ = one beat.

Suppose we make our feet continue to beat up and down at the same speed we have been using for the music we have played so far, but call each down-up motion a *half note* (♩ = one beat). When the composer intends such a state of affairs, he puts a 2 in the place where we have been accustomed to see a 4. In this location it represents the denominator of the fraction ½, and the music would be played as follows:

Ex. 32

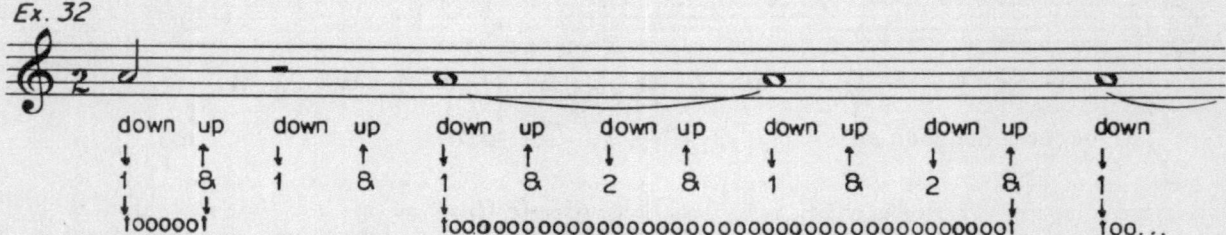

To a listener, the preceding exercise would *sound the same*, and the motions the players go through would *be the same*, as if it were written like this:

Ex. 33

The only difference in these two versions is the way in which they are written on the page. *They are played the same and sound the same.*

Notice that, in the new rhythmic notation, half notes are still one half as long as whole notes, etc. Comparative relationships of this nature are unaffected, therefore, by the choice of which note value is to be designated as "one beat in length".

Ex. 34

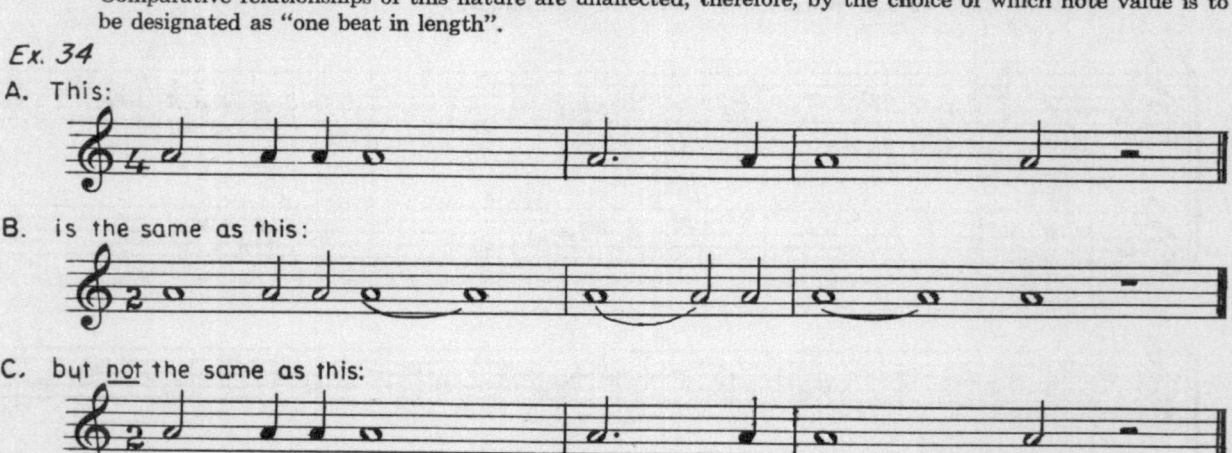

In case of doubt, let it be emphasized again that the foot does not **move** *either* twice as fast or twice as slow in Example B as it does in Example A. It moves at *identically* the same speed for both A and B.

The following exercise will help to familiarize you with the new rhythmic concept:

TEMPO

In playing a certain piece of music, your foot may be going up and down rapidly. If so, it is said that you are playing "at a fast tempo". If your foot moves more slowly, then it is said that "the tempo is slower".

The tempo is independent of whatever note value is being used to represent one beat. Thus, a piece in 2 time may be played at a faster tempo than another piece in 4 time.

CONCLUSION: About Lesson IV

Now, although we still have not mastered the whole art of music, we already know enough to play some pieces which are musically complete and aesthetically satisfying. We have supplied in the following pages a large number of duets which constitute Lesson IV. You should master all of them before going on to learn any further new tones or features of musical notation. These duets will serve to consolidate and crystallize in your mind all of the things we have discussed in the preceding pages. You will then have developed a sureness and confidence that will permit you to enter upon the new material in Lesson V without fear, and your progress will be all the more rapid.

Remember to pay primary attention to your tongue action and to perfecting your ability to read notes. Do not concern yourself over-much with fingerings. You already know ten. There are only seventeen more to learn.

Lesson IV
SEVEN DUETS FOR SOPRANO AND ALTO RECORDERS

Lesson V

TIME VALUES IN MUSIC (Part Two): *Playing Half-Beat Notes*
1. In "Half-Note Time Signatures"

In music which is written with a time signature like $\frac{4}{2}$, the *half note* represents *one beat*, and *the whole note* represents *two beats*. Simple logic tells us that the *quarter note* will then represent *one-half of a beat* — that is, that it will require *two quarter notes* to add up to *one full beat*. What is the means by which this is done in actual practice?

Up to now, we have thought of each note as a "toooot" of calculated length. In approaching now for the first time the problem of notes which are "less than one beat in length", we abbreviate the "toooot" into an indefinitely short "tut", or "t't", with practically no measurable time-lapse between the initial "t" and the final "t".

To play quarter notes in a "half-note time signature", then, we play our notes as short as possible, playing *one note on each down-stroke* of the foot and *another on each up-stroke*:

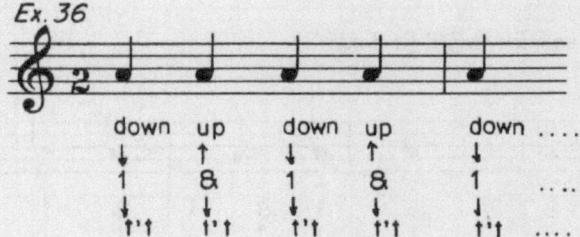

This concept — of notes which are smaller in magnitude than one beat — is very important. Keep playing series of half-beat notes, as above, until you are quite sure of yourself.

Now we combine half-beat notes with longer note values:

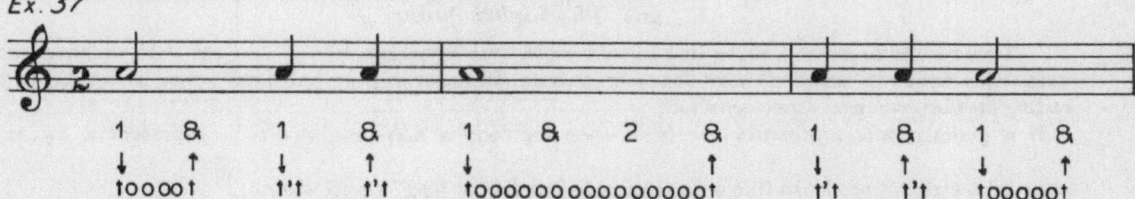

When another note is tied into a half-beat note, the half-beat note really does not have any time length at all, but merely serves to eliminate the silence which the note preceding it would ordinarily have:

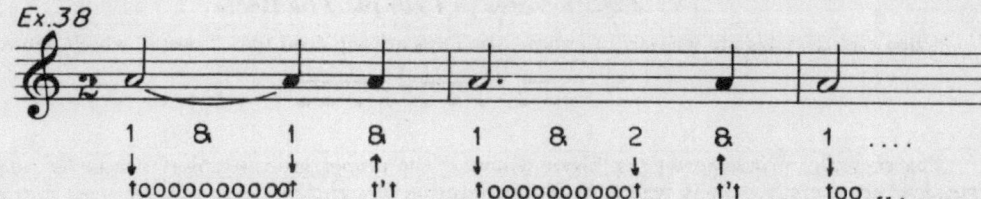

Notice that in the second measure, ♩‿♩ was replaced by its equivalent ♩. . *The two are interpreted identically* as indicated.

In the first measure, the counting is "1 and 1" because there are two separate notes, whereas, in the second measure, there is only one symbol (a dotted half note) to indicate the desired time value; therefore, in the second measure, the counting is "1 and 2".

The general rule is that a dot after a note adds *half again* the apparent time value to the note to which it is attached.

You have played many half notes which begin on the down-stroke and end on the up-stroke. Any half note can equally well begin on an up-stroke and be terminated on the next down-stroke.

When half-beat notes are tied together in the following way, their performance is as shown:

The notation of the preceding example is frequently written like this:

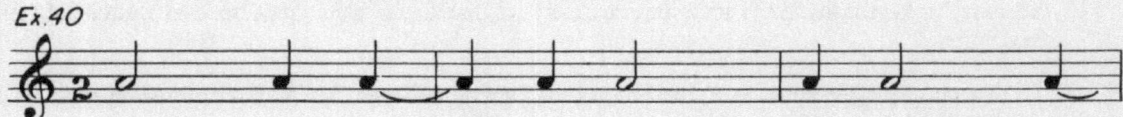

The following exercise would be done:

2. In "Quarter-Note Time Signatures"

(a) The Eighth Note: ♪

If we return to music written in a *quarter-note time signature*, like $\frac{2}{4}$, we see that we have learned no note value which is "smaller" than the quarter note. In order to play half-beat notes, as we did in the preceding section, we need a new symbol.

If a *quarter note* represents *one beat*, then logically a *half-beat* would be represented by an *eighth note*. The eighth note looks like a quarter note but has a "flag" on its stem: ♪

(b) Eighth Notes in Groups; The Beam: ⌐

When eighth notes are written in groups, the flags are replaced by a "beam" which connects the stems:

♫, ♫♪, ♫♫

The examples which were given above, showing the proper interpretation of *quarter notes in half-note time signatures*, apply equally well to the interpretation of *eighth notes in quarter-note time signatures*.

Play the following:

(c) The Eighth Rest: ⁷

The rest value corresponding to the eighth note is the *eighth rest*, notated this way: ⁷

The following would be interpreted:

Ex. 43

In this example, the first few notes (♩ ♫) could be written as ♩. ♪, following the same logic as ♩ ♩ = ♩.

SUMMARY: *Three Duets*

1.

Lesson VI

HALF-HOLE TECHNIQUE: *Extending Our Range Upward:*

In order to learn our next fingerings, it is necessary to return momentarily to the very first note which we learned. Play:

Keep this exact same fingering, but shift the left-hand thumb so that it leaves about half of the thumb-hole open. This should be done by holding the thumb in such a way that the thumb-nail will provide a comparatively solid, tough wall to match the wooden wall of the edge of the hole itself:

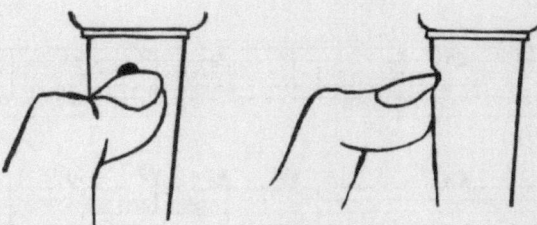

Place the thumb at a slight angle in order to permit a natural hand position. Do *not* hold it at a *right angle* to the thumb-hole.

With the fingers in the same position, but with the thumb held in the way just described, give a clear, clean attack with the tongue, and blow:

Many people encounter difficulty when they first attempt this note. The first thing to consider is the half-hole thumb. Beginning with this note, and for all notes above it (which we will be learning shortly), the amount of the hole you leave uncovered is very important. Therefore, you must experiment. Shift your thumb around. Try leaving just a tiny crack or   If that doesn't work, try leaving a large opening. You will soon hit on the right combination.

Breath pressure is also important. If you do not blow hard enough, no thumb or finger position in the world will serve to produce this tone for you. On the other hand, too much breath pressure will produce a squawk and various high squeak-noises.

To get used to the idea of producing notes using this new thumb position, play the new note in alternation with the lower one several times:

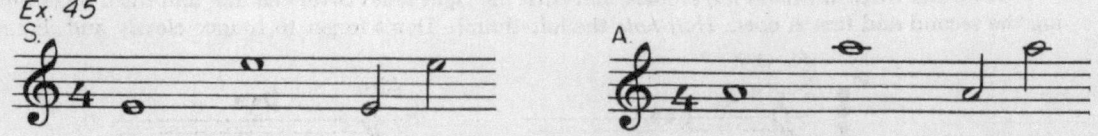

Make certain that none of your idle fingers is hovering too near any hole that is supposed to be open. You may impede the free flow of air out of that hole, and upset the delicate equilibrium inside the recorder.

SOME REMARKS ABOUT FINGER POSITION

While on the subject, this may be an opportune time to mention a few general precautions regarding the various fingers when they are temporarily idle.

If you are playing a note which requires only left-hand fingers, be sure to keep the right hand roughly in its correct place, so that if you suddenly had to play the very lowest note on the instrument, you would need only to drop each idle finger about one inch or so straight down onto its respective fingerhole. It is very important to guard against bunching idle fingers up, far away from the holes which they regulate, so that each note must be painstakingly groped for. You will never attain proficiency on your instrument if you have to take time to grope for each note.

You must also avoid the opposite mistake of making each finger hover right over its hole, barely a quarter-inch away. As previously pointed out, this will impede the free flow of air, and upset the delicate equilibrium inside the instrument. The correct procedure is to hold idle fingers directly over the holes they regulate, about an inch above. From this convenient position, they can drop into place as required, with no difficulty at all. A good exercise to develop this habit is:

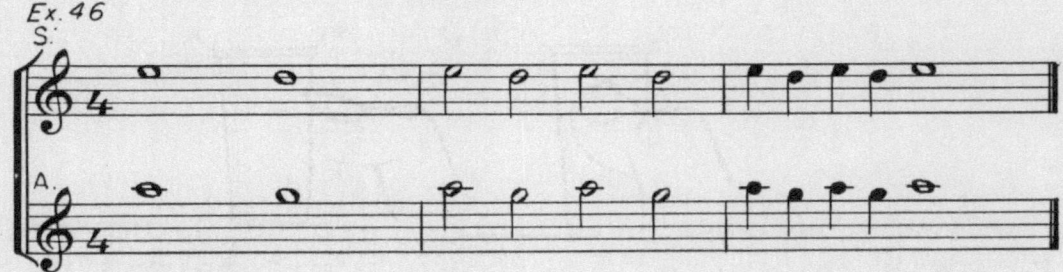

Play the sequence of tones which follows:

FOUR HIGHER NOTES:

Now we proceed to several higher tones.

Cover the three left-hand fingerholes, and with the right hand cover the first and third fingerholes, leaving the second and fourth open. *Half-hole* the left thumb. Don't forget to tongue clearly and distinctly.

Now play this new tone in alternation with the low note:

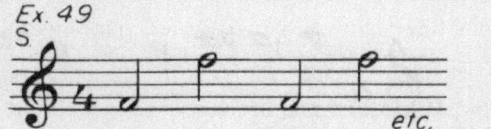
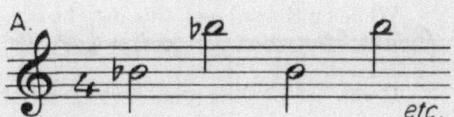

Now an exercise using this note with its adjacent neighbors:

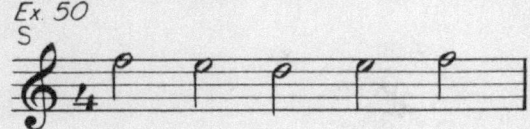
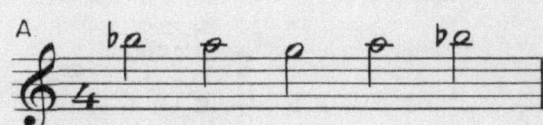

For the next new note, allow the left hand to keep the same position, but let the right hand cover the *second hole only*, leaving the first, third, and fourth holes open. Be sure that the position of the *half-hole* thumb is used and that you tongue clearly:

An exercise in alternation with its low note:

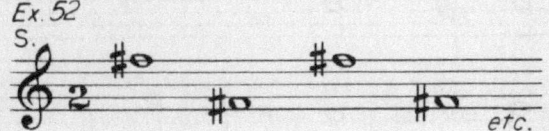

And with its adjacent neighbors:

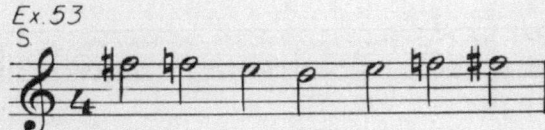
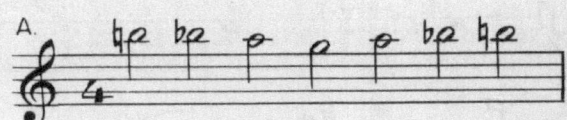

Now uncover all right-hand notes, letting the left hand remain the same — namely, the three holes covered and the half-hole position — and we have another tone:

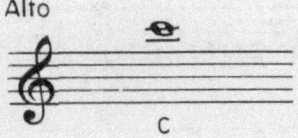

Use no post for these upper notes of the left hand; use it only for their corresponding lower notes.

Exercise in alternation with its low note:

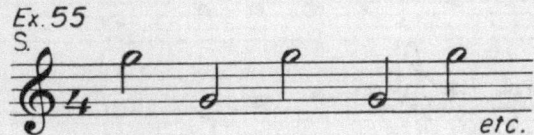

With its adjacent neighbors:

Ex. 56

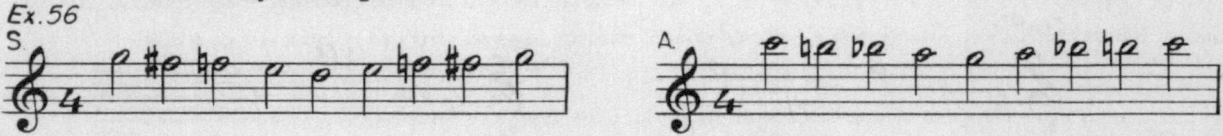

One more step upward: Cover the first two holes with the left hand. Half-hole the thumb and keep all right-hand holes open:

Ex. 57

In combination with its adjacent neighbors and low note:

Ex. 58

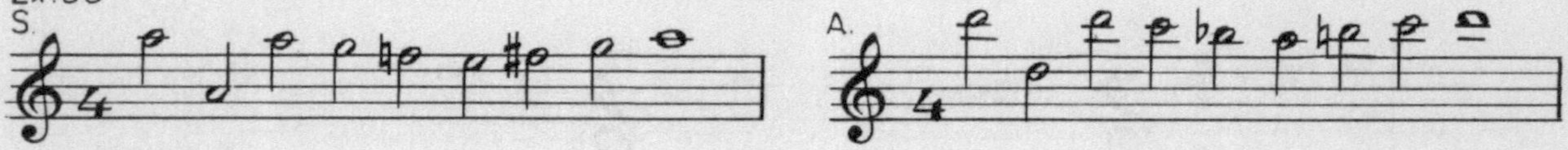

TWO DUETS

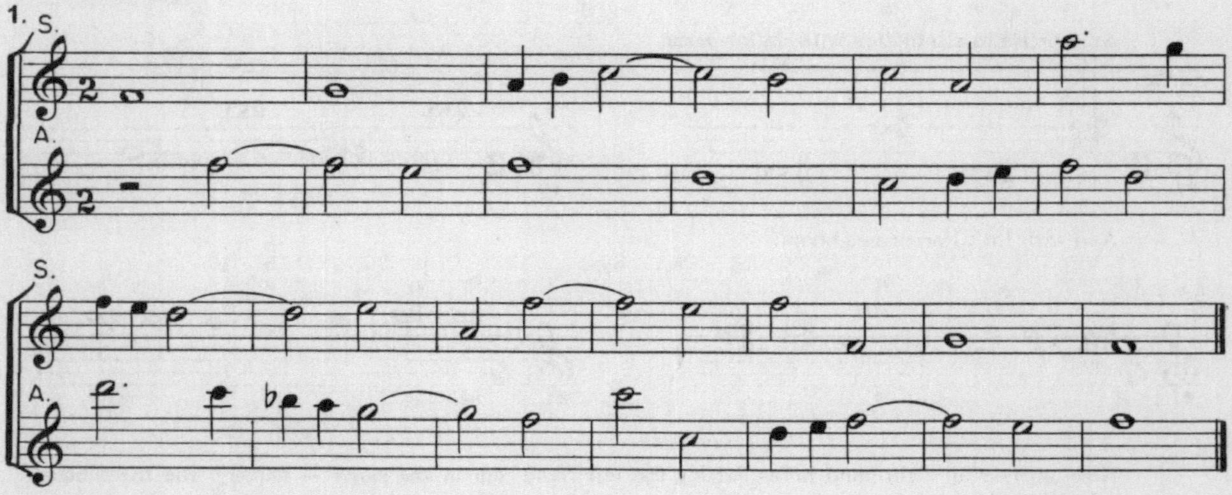

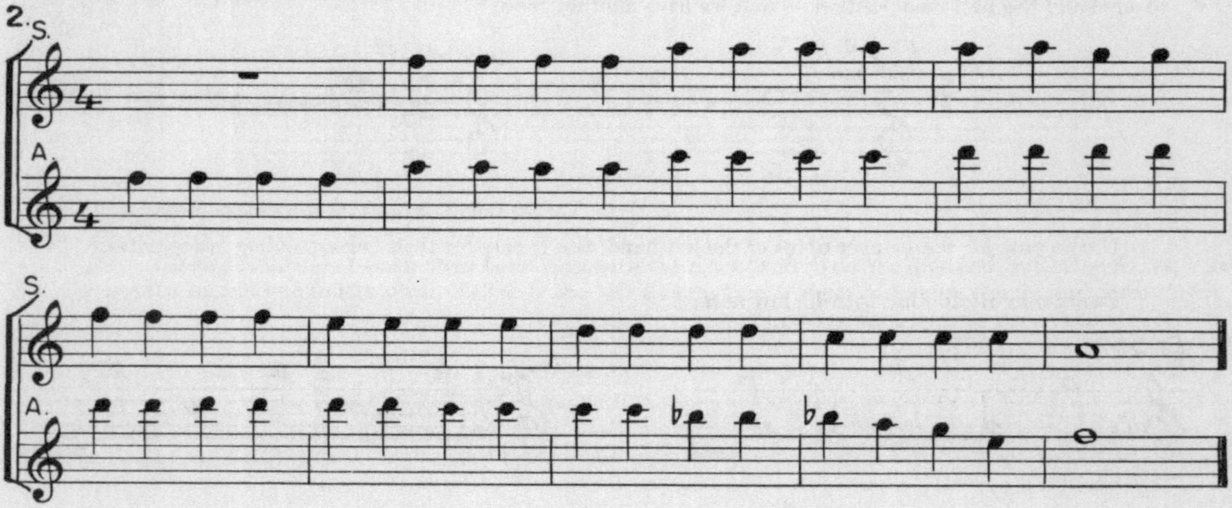

AN INTRODUCTION TO THE C MAJOR SCALE

Play:

Ex. 59

F G A G F A F

Then:

Ex. 60

F G A G F A F

Both of these fragments sound the same in character, and corresponding notes in the two exercises bear the same letter names. We have here an explanation of a phenomenon which you may have noticed in the preceding pages: All the notes in music are called by the letters of the alphabet, but only the first seven are used — A, B, C, D, E, F, and G. The degrees of the music staff bear those letter names in alphabetical order proceeding upward, and when we pass "G", the next degree is "A" again, as in the following:

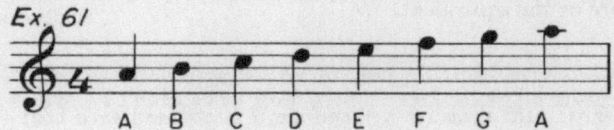

A B C D E F G A

The upper "A" sounds like a sort of "mirror image" of the lower "A". The high "A" is called the *upper octave* of the lower "A", and the lower "A" is called the *lower octave* of the higher "A". The two "A's" are said to be an *octave apart*.

Going back to the two exercises at the beginning of this section, the two series of F, G, A, G, F, etc. sounded similar in character because one was an *octave duplication*, or *octave reflection* of the other. This phenomenon of octave duplication makes it possible for us to summarize all of the natural notes in music in a compact way, by means of what we call the "C major scale". It is written and played as follows:

The *C major scale* or *scale of C major* (as it may also be called) is not the only "major scale". A major scale may be constructed starting with any musical tone whatever as its point of beginning. It happens that when the major scale begins on C, there are no accidentals (sharps or flats) involved; whereas a major scale beginning on any tone other than C *does* require the use of accidentals to maintain the special relationships (spacing) between the scale notes.

The exact meaning of this will become clear a few lessons hence, after we have actually played several other scales. But for the moment, it will be helpful to remember that the letter names of all scales proceed in alphabetical order, regardless of accidentals. Do not try to play any other scale but the C major scale as played just previously. We will go no deeper into scale study now, but will wait until a later lesson, after we have learned several new fingerings.

ABOUT MEASURES AND TIME SIGNATURES

There is not much that is new to be covered in this lesson as far as rhythm is concerned. Our only concern at this point will be to show how, in frequent instances, music may be written with bar-lines written at regular intervals.

Suppose, in a musical example which is written with the quarter note as its one-beat unit, a bar-line is used to mark off *every 4th beat*:

Ex. 63

When bar-lines are regularly spaced in this way, we call that portion of the musical staff enclosed by two adjacent bar-lines a *measure*. This term, measure, is used here in the same sense as when we portion out equal quantities of grain. A measure of grain implies equal portions out of a large store or supply — similarly with equal measures in music.

A music measure need not necessarily contain four beats, nor need the beats be quarter-note beats. In order to show how many beats are to be contained in each measure, and what note value is to represent a beat, we write *two* numbers at the beginning of the music, one above the other:

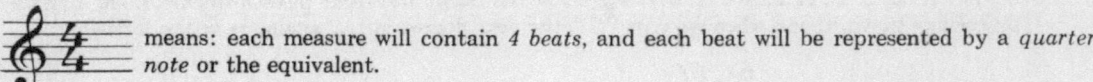
means: each measure will contain *4 beats*, and each beat will be represented by a *quarter note* or the equivalent.

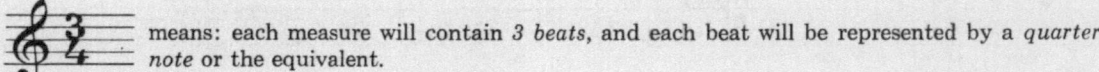
means: each measure will contain *3 beats*, and each beat will be represented by a *quarter note* or the equivalent.

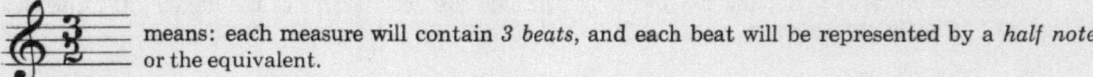
means: each measure will contain *3 beats*, and each beat will be represented by a *half note* or the equivalent.

Here are four examples of different time signatures:

The upper number, then, tells how many beats there are in each measure, and the lower number tells what note value is being used to represent a single beat. (We commonly say that, in 3/4 or 4/4 time, the quarter note "gets the beat".)

Analyze the following time signatures:

$$\frac{13}{4} \quad \frac{6}{2} \quad \frac{9}{2} \quad \frac{6}{4} \quad \frac{4}{2} \quad \frac{4}{4} \quad \frac{9}{1}$$

Most of the music you encounter will be written with regularly spaced bar-lines. It is therefore important to remember what we have said before: that the bar-lines are not important to the player, and should be ignored as far as actual playing is concerned. They can be of use; e.g., if it is desired to begin playing in the middle of a piece of music, the members of the ensemble can count measures to arrive at a certain place where they want to begin playing. But the actual "counting" of music should be done independently of the bar-lines.

MUSICAL TERMINOLOGY: *Some Further Observations*

Earlier, we spoke of an ambiguity in musical terminology which was caused by the careless use of the word "beat". Strictly speaking, "beat" refers to an impact, but we sometimes speak of the *time lapse between two adjacent* beats, calling that *space of time* a beat.

A similar ambiguity arises with music measures, which are sometimes referred to as "bars". Thus, as explained in a previous lesson, two lines drawn across the staff constitute a *double bar;* a single line drawn across the staff is called a *bar-line;* that which is contained between two bar-lines (or between a bar-line and double bar) is a measure but *may* also be called "a bar"!

Once again, all we can do is to point out the ambiguity and to state that you, like all other musicians, are going to have to "live with it".

Most of the music in the pages following will be written with regularly spaced bar-lines, but there will be some written without them — so keep away from growing dependent on them.

A DUET IN 3/4 TIME

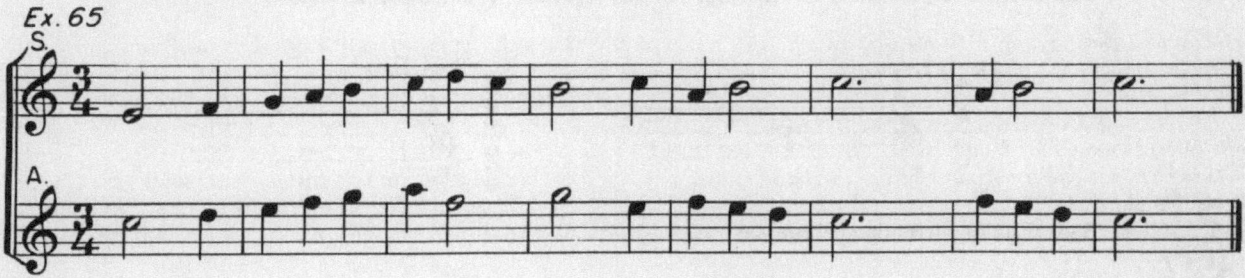

Lesson VII

THE G MAJOR SCALE (The Altos Learn F♯: 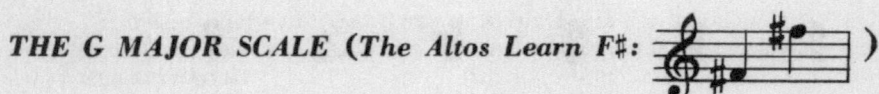)

The sopranos have previously learned to play F♯. The altos must now learn it:

[∅ signifies a hole only partly covered. You must experiment with the exact amount to cover.]

With both sizes of recorder able to play F♯, we can introduce the first scale which calls for notes other than natural notes—the scale of G major, so called because it begins and ends on G:

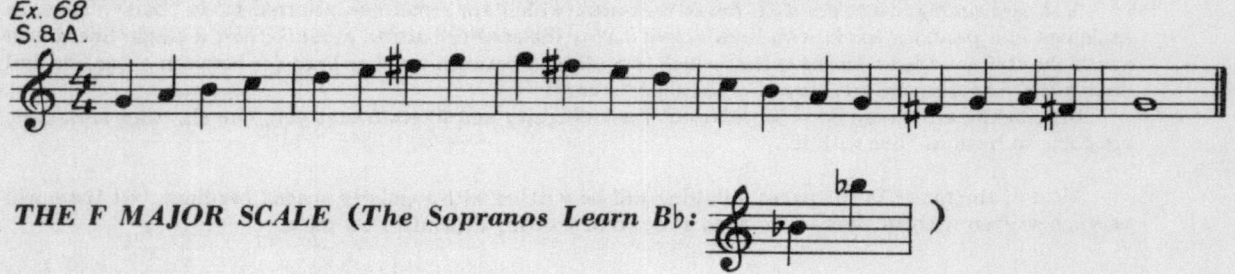

THE F MAJOR SCALE (The Sopranos Learn B♭: 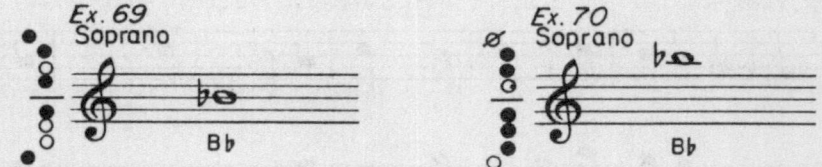)

The altos have previously learned B♭. For the sopranos, it is written as follows:

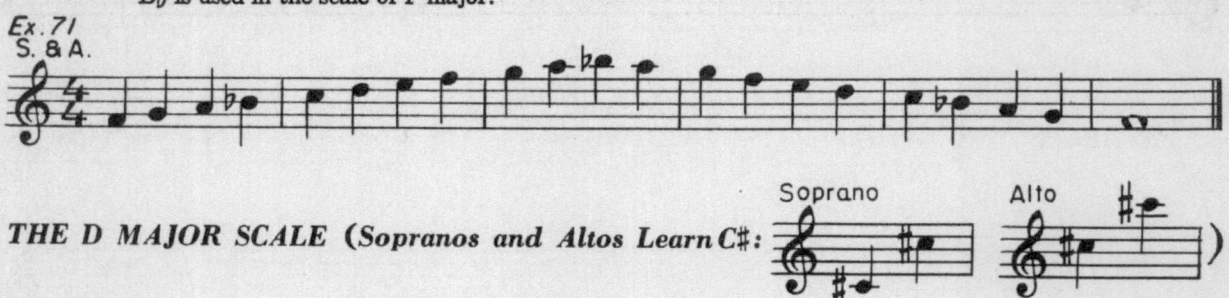

B♭ is used in the scale of F major:

THE D MAJOR SCALE (Sopranos and Altos Learn C♯: )

Now everyone will learn C♯:

C♯ is used in the scale of D major:

ABOUT KEYS AND KEY SIGNATURES

1. *G Major*

Most music is so written that it makes consistent use of the notes of a certain scale. If a composition keeps predominantly to the notes of the *G major scale*, the composition is said to be "written in the key of G major". In such a case, since the scale of G major includes an F♯ but no F♮, it follows that a composition "written in the key of G major" will require more F♯'s to be played than F♮'s. In order to save much extra labor involved in inserting ♯ signs into the text of the music, *a ♯ sign is put on the staff at the beginning of each line of music:*

Ex. 75

This sharp sign applies to *all* F's, in *every* octave. It is therefore not necessary to write , for the sharp on the top line takes care of every octave.

When a sharp is employed in this way, it called a *key signature*, just as a designation like 4/4 is called a "time signature". Such a sharp, written as a key signature, applies to all F's in the entire composition, and says they should all be played as F♯'s.

If an F♮ is desired for a certain note, a ♮ sign must be written in front of it. The ♯ which constitutes the key signature is not called an "accidental", but a ♮ used occasionally at various points in the text to contradict the key signature *is* called an accidental. When such a contradiction does occur, *it applies to all notes on that degree of the scale which appear following it within the same measure.*

In the following example, the exact note names are given below the staff in order to show exactly what would be done:

2. *F Major*

When a composition is written in *F major*, the B♭ will more often be needed than the B♮. The B♭ can be incorporated into the key signature just as the F♯ was in the previous example:

3. D Major

The scale of D major, and thus compositions written in D major, make consistent use both of F♯ and C♯. *Both* appear in the key signature:

Ex. 78

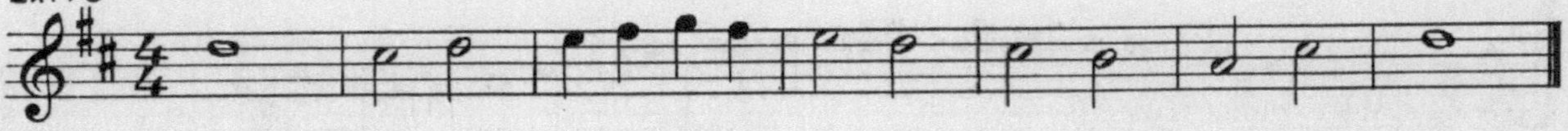

SUMMARY: *The Scales of C, G, F and D Major*

We summarize by writing all four scales which you have so far learned. The ♯'s and the ♭'s no longer appear directly in front of their respective notes, but have been put into the key signature.

Ex. 79 C Major

Ex. 80 G Major

Ex. 81 D Major

Ex. 82 F Major

Lesson VIII

TWO NEW SYMBOLS

1. *The Repeat Sign:* 𝄇 *or* 𝄆

A symbol which is of utmost importance is the *repeat sign:* 𝄇

Music written in the following way:

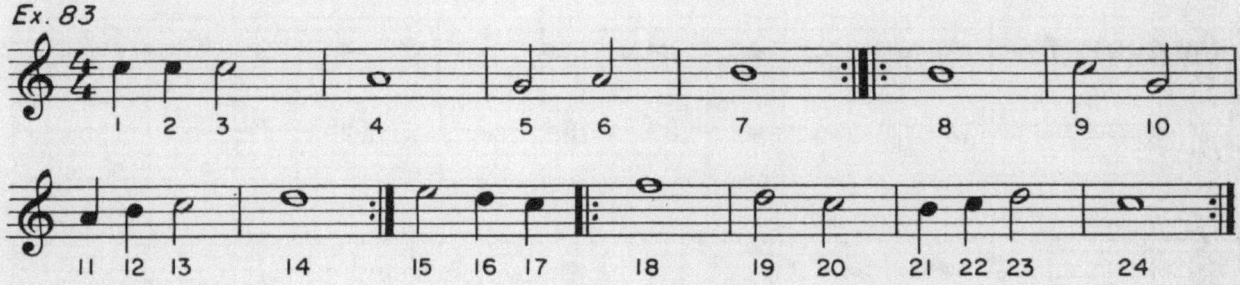

would be interpreted as follows:

The first four measures would be played as usual, from note #1 to note #7; but immediately after note #7, without any pause, note #1 is played again, and the whole first four measures are repeated until note #7 is again reached, whereupon note #8 immediately follows, and so on to note #14.

Again, without any pause after the conclusion of note #14, note #8 is played and the second section thus repeated, until note #14 is reached for the second time.

Note #15 then follows immediately and so on to note #17.

Note #18 follows, thence to note #24, then back to #18 to repeat the section, ending finally with the arrival for the second time at note #24.

Notice that all sections meant to be repeated have a repeat sign *both at the beginning and at the end of the section.* The repeat sign at the beginning has the dots on the right side of the double bar, and the repeat sign at the end of the section has the dots on the left side. The only exception is that when the first section of a piece is to be repeated, no repeat sign is necessary at the very beginning. The reason for this is that when the player arrives at the first repeat sign, as at measure 4 above, there can be no doubt where to go back to.

2. Repeated ("Slashed") Notes

Various note values sometimes appear with a slash through their stems, or if they have no stems, immediately below the note head.

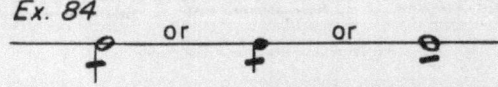

This slash signifies that a series of eighth notes are to be played, sufficient in number to "add up" arithmetically to the "total time value" indicated by the note which bears the slash:

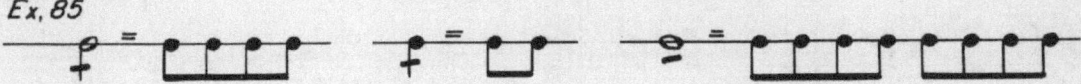

ELEVEN DUETS, INCLUDING MUSIC IN 6/8 AND 3/8

The repeat sign and "slashed notes" will appear in the following duets, which have been designed to increase your facility before proceeding to more new material. We must again admonish you to concern yourself primarily with rhythm and articulation, not worrying overmuch about fingerings. You now know eighteen fingerings, and there are only nine more to be learned.

Several of the time signatures have an 8 in the denominator $\frac{3}{8}$ and $\frac{6}{8}$. Remember that each eighth note should commence on a "down" and terminate on the following "up", just like a quarter note in 4/4 time. All other values would be treated accordingly (a dotted quarter note equals three beats, a half note equals four, a quarter note equals two, etc.)

7. "Parson's Farewell"

8.

9.

Lesson IX

TIME VALUES IN MUSIC (Part Three): The Sixteenth Note 𝅘𝅥𝅯 and Rest 𝄿

1. *Playing Sixteenth Notes:* 𝅘𝅥𝅯𝅘𝅥𝅯, 𝅘𝅥𝅯𝅘𝅥𝅯𝅘𝅥𝅯𝅘𝅥𝅯, *etc.*

In this lesson, we discuss the proper execution of sixteenth notes. The first thing that should be said about sixteenth notes is that *they are not played rapidly*. Many beginners have an almost superstitious fear of them, because of the large amount of popular propaganda which characterizes them (along with all the smaller note values) as "black notes."

For our first exercise, let your foot tap at a moderate speed and play this series of sixteenth notes:

Ex. 86

According to the method of performance indicated above, one extra note is to be sandwiched between every two consecutive motions of the foot. Each sixteenth note is to be indefinitely short — just as eighth notes are indefinitely short. Note that the up-stroke occurs on the third sixteenth in a group of four sixteenths.

2. *Combinations: Sixteenth Notes and Rests; Sixteenths and Eighths*

This brings us to the very important principle that the eighth note and the sixteenth note *are both of the same length*: the only difference is that sixteenth notes have *a smaller time-lapse* between them.

Suppose, for example, that we begin with several groups of *four* sixteenths and, at a certain point, start omitting the second note of each group, making use of the *sixteenth rest* 𝄿 to indicate the missing note:

Ex. 87

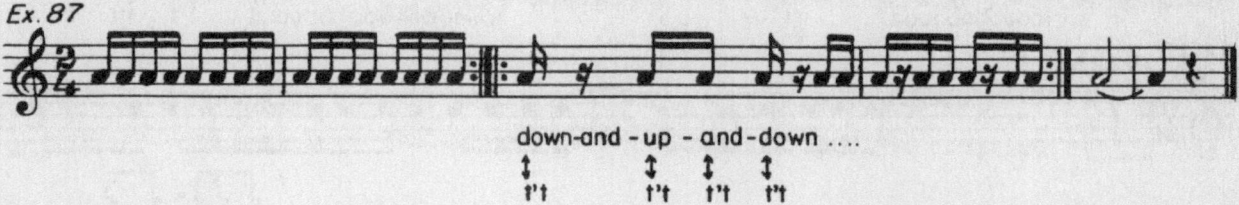

The following exercise would be played (and would sound to a listener) *identically* the same as the preceding one:

Ex. 88

In other words, ♪♫ is just another way of writing ♪𝄽♫ : both stand for the same thing. By the same logic ♫♫𝄽 = ♫♫ :

Ex. 89

* 𝄽 = ♫♫

Play the figures ♪𝄽♫ (♪♫) and ♫♫𝄽 (♫♫) over and over until they become second nature. Then practice leaving out the *third* note of each group:

Ex. 90

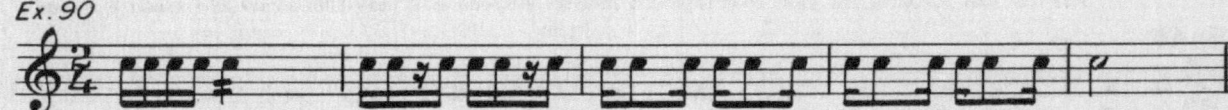

Again ♫♫𝄽♪ = ♫♫♪ Both sound the same.

Now leave out the *first* note of each group:

Ex. 91

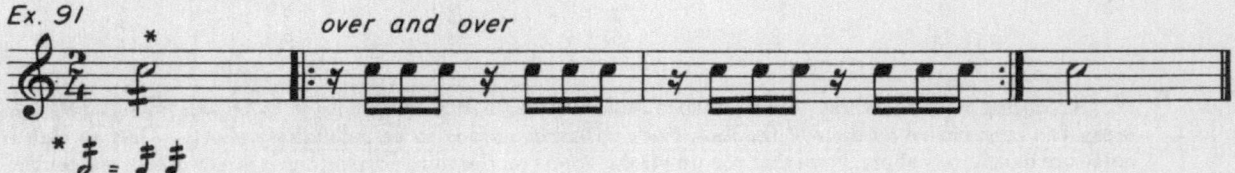

* 𝄽 = 𝄽𝄽

3. Tying the Sixteenth Note

The treatment of sixteenth notes which are tied to other notes is similar to that which we learned in the case of eighth notes. Here is how they compare:

Do the following exercises on the pitch of C:

Ex. 96

SUMMARY: Three Duets and a Scale Exercise

*The symbol ∕. means to repeat the preceding bar.

Lesson X

TWO NEW NOTES:

Our first task in this lesson is to learn two fingerings:

THREE NEW SCALES: B♭ Major, E♭ Major and A Major

These two fingerings are needed in the two following scales:

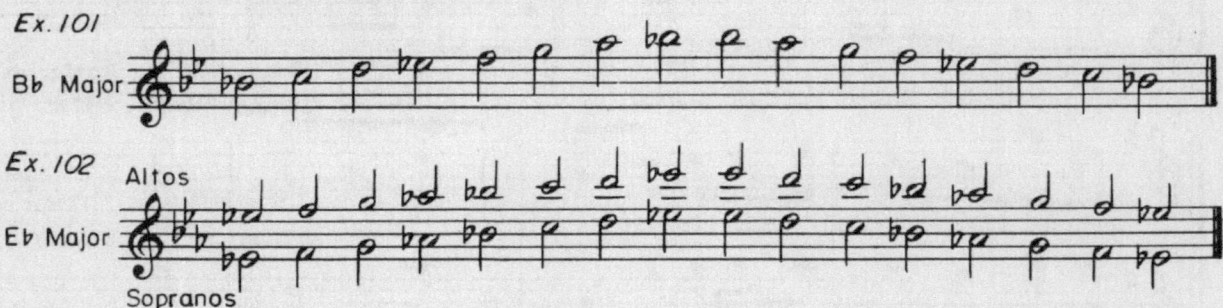

It so happens that the fingering you just used to play A♭ is also used to play G♯. In other words, A♭ and G♯ *are one and the same tone with two different names.*

G♯ is used in the scale of A major:

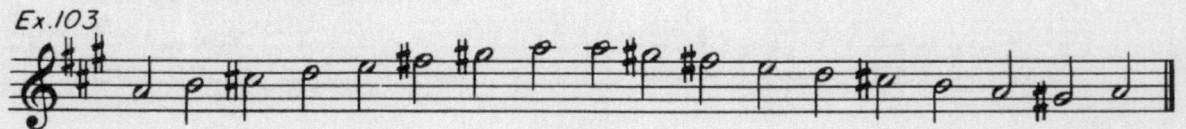

THE CHROMATIC SCALE

You now know enough fingerings to play the following sequence of notes:

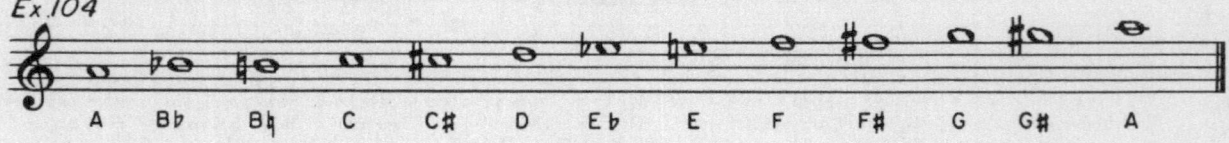

This sequence is called the *chromatic scale*. It represents an ordered collection of all possible musical tones within the octave marked off by the *lower* A and the *upper* A*. The chromatic scale need not begin with A; one might begin with any tone. The only requirement is that all possible tones should be present between the tone upon which you begin and the upper octave of that tone.

THE NAMING OF NOTE PITCHES

You have probably noticed that the *names* of the various tones do not seem to follow any consistent order. For instance, there is a C♯ but no E♯; a B♭ but no A♭, etc. We will attempt some sort of explanation.

There was a time when the notes which comprise the C major scale were the only ones known and used in Europe. They were named in alphabetical order,

A B C D E F G

Later, five other tones came into use. One of them was higher than A but lower than B, and so was called either "A-sharp" or "B-flat". Another tone lies between C and D, and bears the names "C-sharp" and/or "D-flat". The other three intermediate tones are: D-sharp = E-flat, F-sharp = G-flat, and G-sharp = A-flat. (No tones have ever come into common use which lie midway between B and C or between E and F.)

Let us now write the chromatic scale in such a way as to show all note names:

Ex.105

A A♯ B♭ B C C♯ D♭ D D♯ E♭ E F F♯ G♭ G G♯ A♭ . A

Musicians have framed the general rule: "D-sharp is that tone which lies next *above* D-natural in the chromatic scale, and D-flat is that tone which lies next *below* D-natural in the chromatic scale." This is only one specific example; the same rule holds true for the other natural tones.

Because of the peculiarities of this system of notation, it will be seen that the *fingering* for B-sharp is the same as the fingering for C-natural, and C-flat is fingered like B-natural. In the same way, E-sharp is equivalent to F-natural and F-flat is equivalent to E-natural.

Occasionally, you will see a *double-flat* symbol: ♭♭, or a *double-sharp* symbol: x ;   Cx = D♮, G♭♭ = F♮, etc. By this logic, Bx would be the same as C♯, and F♭♭ = E♭, etc.

---

*The word "possible" should be taken to mean "available to us" in the context of this book. String and wind instruments are capable of producing fine gradations of pitch even smaller than the half-step. The study of these "microtones" need not concern us in our present course.

Lesson XI

TIME VALUES IN MUSIC (Part Four): Smaller Note Values

1. The Thirty-Second Note and Rest

♪ is an *eighth* note (1/8)

♫ is a *sixteenth* note (1/16)

is a *thirty-second* note (1/32)

is a *sixty-fourth* note (1/64)
(and so on)

By the above, you see that the denominator of the fraction *doubles* with each added "flag".

In any given tempo and rhythm, if an 1/8-note is a *half*-beat in length, then the 1/16-note is a *quarter*-beat in length, the 1/32-note is an *eighth*-beat in length, etc.

The rest value corresponding to a given note value always has the same number of flags:

𝄾 is an *eighth* rest

is a *sixteenth* rest

is a *thirty-second* rest

is a *sixty-fourth* rest
(and so on)

It is *most important* to remember that these smaller note values are not necessarily difficult to play. It is especially true of sixteenth notes in 4/4 time, that they are usually quite leisurely in execution, especially when the foot-beat is quite slow and deliberate. At a slow rate of speed, it is surprising how many notes can be played within the space of time from one beat to the next.

Try playing a series of sixteenth notes at an ordinary rate of speed:

(As usual, the "down-ups" indicate the proper foot motion.)

Now play the same string of sixteenth notes, but do not let your foot move up and down as often. (This may be tricky at first, but *make* your foot stay on the floor until it is time to snap up.)
You now are playing:

Notice the change in time signature. You are playing the same series of notes as before, but your foot moves down and up only once for every eight sixteenth notes. Eight sixteenth notes "add up" to one half note. You are "beating" half notes, and are *playing* eight notes for every beat. This sounds like a difficult feat, but you know it is not, *for you have merely cut your foot motion in half*. You have not "sped up" your playing at all.

Now let us play the same series of notes again, with the *same speed* for our down-up foot motions. But let us write out the notation on paper in such a way that we have eight notes per beat in $\frac{4}{4}$ time. *Each note is now called a thirty-second note:*

This is the same series of notes we played before, and to any listener the sound is identical. But when done with this kind of foot-beat and corresponding notation, the music looks incredibly difficult. The page is filled with "black notes" — those legendary, exotic, mysterious things supposed to be the exclusive property of great virtuosi whose "inborn talent" enables them, and them alone, to understand and to execute them. By playing these last exercises you have personally demonstrated the absurdity of such ideas. You may be interested to know that you can now speed up your thirty-second notes beyond the speed at which you just played them. Try it, but do not go so fast that your tongue motion loses its control. Later, you will do thirty-second notes faster, as soon as you learn "slurring".

2. *The Sixteenth-Note Triplet:*

If you can play *eight* notes in the space of one beat, presumably it must not be too difficult to play only *six*. Remember to make each note as short as you can:

This example involves the use of grouplets — *three sixteenth notes in each* — in a place where we would ordinarily expect to find *pairs* of sixteenths. The symbol ⌐3¬ indicates the idea of *three equally-spaced notes which take up exactly as much time as two notes of the same value.*

The logic of this should cause no difficulty if you remember that there was once a time in musical history when the rule said: "Each whole note can be divided into *either* two *or* three half notes, each half note into two *or* three quarters,, and so with all other values."

Therefore, a "triplet" with a given number of beams should be given the same total amount of time as an ordinary duple pair with the same number of beams:

                 ♪♪♪ (3)   occupies the same amount of time as   ♪♪

                 ♪♪♪ (3)   occupies the same amount of time as   ♪♪

                 ♪♪♪ (3)   occupies the same amount of time as   ♪♪

SOME COMMON SHORT-NOTE PATTERNS

In playing series of notes like:

A.

B.

we can leave out all but the first and last of each grouplet:

This is more often expressed as:

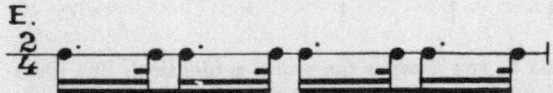 

But the execution is the same. (Remember that notes shorter than one beat are indefinitely short.) Usually, there is no discernable difference between ♩ and ♪ . Each is the musical equivalent of the spoken word "*A-hem*". There is no definite time value given to the "A". It is just a short sound immediately preceding the longer sound, "hem". Orchestra conductors pronounce "tump-ta-tump-ta-tump-" etc. when trying to transmit to the players how they want such figures played.

Another frequent figure is: ♪ . The verbal interpretation is "Tump-ta-ta-tump-ta-ta ..." In other words, two short notes immediately preceding a longer one.

Such figures as:

  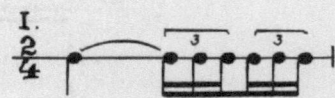

which involve ties terminating in short note values, should be performed according to the principles learned in previous pages. For example:

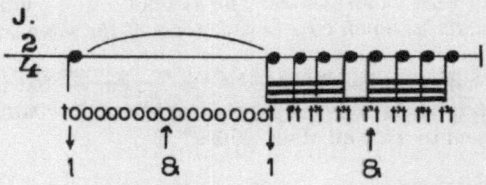

Lesson XII

TEMPO AND RHYTHM (METER)

The rhythmic techniques we have learned so far are applicable to all music in which the foot beats fairly slowly — or, as we say, when the *tempo* is leisurely. *Tempo*, then, refers to the relative speed of the foot-motion and is expressed in "beats per minute."

All the music we have played so far has been executed in "tempi" of between 30 and 70 beats each minute. As we have seen, the speed of motion of the foot (i.e., the tempo) has no relationship to the rhythm of a musical selection. For instance, we may have played one piece in $\frac{4}{2}$ time (a "half-note rhythm") at a tempo of 60 beats per minute, after which we may have played another piece in $\frac{4}{4}$ time (a "quarter-note rhythm") at a tempo of 40 beats per minute. In such a case, the quarter note would occupy a greater absolute length of time in the second piece than did the half note in the first piece. For any one given piece of music, however, there is a definite relationship between the "rhythm"* and the tempo which remains constant throughout the piece.

In the two examples we have just talked about, this relationship can be expressed as follows:

$$(a) \quad \frac{4}{2} \quad \bd = 60 \qquad\qquad (b) \quad \frac{4}{4} \quad \qd = 40$$

In example (a), the time signature shows the rhythm to be $\frac{4}{2}$ (4 beats in each measure, each beat represented by a half note). The symbol $\bd = 60$ may be written above the staff near the beginning of the piece to show that the tempo is to be approximately 60 beats per minute. $\bd = 60$ makes it clear that each beat is represented by a $\bd$. The situation is similar in example (b).

An indication like $\bd = 60$ looks quite scientific and exact. In actual fact, it is only meant as an approximation, and different players may vary this according to taste. Both in matters of rhythm and in matters of tempo, composers have traditionally been quite careless. Many times a piece will bear the numbers $\frac{4}{4}$ at the beginning, but will sound best when played as if the signature were $\frac{2}{2}$. In other words, it will sound better to "beat half notes" than to "beat quarter notes".

The following material will clarify how this is possible, but for the moment, let it be said in defense of the composers that there is no real need to be precise about tempo and rhythm designations, the speed at which a given piece of music is played being ordinarily left to the taste and discretion of the people performing it. We could send a piece of music to a group of musicians in Australia, stripped of all tempo indications and with all time signatures removed; then give the same music, similarly divested of rhythm and tempo indications, to another group here in North America. If the two bands of musicians rehearsed the music, each according to the dictates of its own sense of taste, and if the two groups were then brought together, it would be found in most cases that they were within, say, 10 to 15 beats per minute of the same tempo, and would almost invariably be using the same note value as the one-beat unit! In other words, the correct rhythm and tempo for any given piece practically *suggest themselves* to the well-trained musician, and there is no need for great exactness in tempo or rhythm indications.

Perhaps the best way to summarize this point is as follows:

$\frac{4}{2}$ can be expressed $\overset{4}{\bd}$, and means that each measure contains *4 half notes*.

$\frac{3}{8}$ can be expressed $\overset{3}{\eighthnote}$, and means that each measure contains *3 eighth notes*.

$\frac{6}{1}$ can be expressed $\overset{6}{o}$, and means each measure contains *6 whole notes*.

---

*Some modern authorities refer to the rhythm of a composition as its "meter".

Beyond this, the time signature tells us nothing. The piece in $\overset{6}{1}$ time may be so written that it sounds best at a speed which renders it very convenient to tap the foot twelve times in each measure. Thus, each tap would be represented by a half note or the equivalent, and a more accurate representation of the time signature would be $\overset{12}{1}$ or $\overset{12}{2}$. The composer wrote the "wrong" time signature purely out of carelessness, and the only confusion which could possibly arise would stem from an unawareness on the part of a player of the composer's blasé attitude. Such a player might suppose that the composer's intention could have been none other than literally $\overset{6}{1}$, and might accordingly saddle himself with an awkward foot-motion which might hinder him from a "natural" interpretation of the music.

As we said previously, all the music we have played so far has been at a tempo of about 70 beats per minute or slower. It is perhaps significant that the average "tempo" of the human heart is in this general vicinity. At any rate, when we pass this rate of speed and go on to a more advanced tempo — say, 80 to 90 beats per minute, it becomes difficult to mark off an accurately spaced up-beat. Nor does it sound good to do so. The natural tendency at this speed is to make the foot spring up immediately, as if one were beating on a hot stove rather than on the floor:

When this kind of speed is reached, and the foot springs up in this fashion, it becomes more pleasing to the ear to make *quarter notes indefinitely short*. The reason for this is that the musical ear is no longer hearing quarter notes as one-beat entities. The sound is the same as if you were playing in $\frac{2}{2}$ time with $\textit{d}$ = 40 !!! That is, when the tempo increases to the point that the foot springs up immediately, we are on the threshold of that speed where it is becoming more convenient to beat *according to the next "larger" note value*.

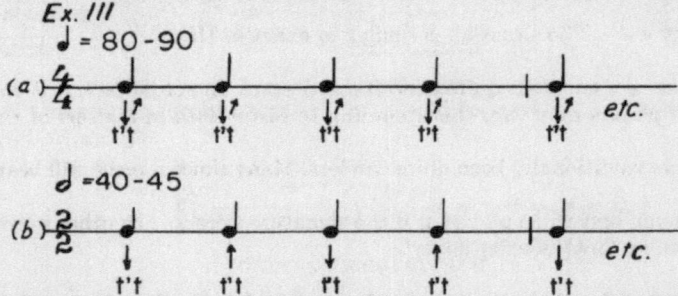

If we remember that the composer could have been careless about his time designation, and used either $\frac{4}{4}$ or $\frac{2}{2}$ for either (a) or (b), we note that both examples are *identical in sound* and *identical in appearance on paper*. The only difference is in the motion of the foot . . . at this particular tempo purely a matter of taste. Neither $\frac{4}{4}$, nor $\frac{2}{2}$, nor $\frac{1}{1}$ for that matter, indicates any other thing than that each measure contains exactly "one whole note's worth of notes."

You should now go back to Lesson VIII and play all the duets at a speed of about 90 beats per minute.

Remember that when ♩ = 90, execution is as follows:

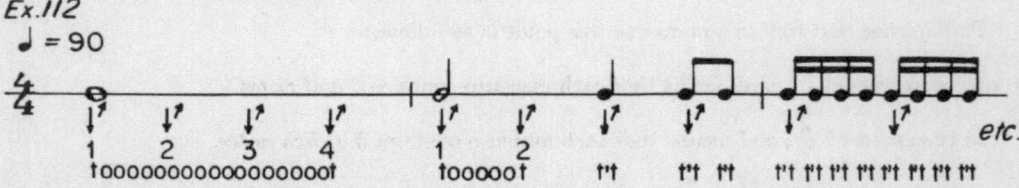

This is precisely what one would do when "beating half notes" at a slower tempo (♩ = 45).

In going through the duets in Lesson VIII, you will note that those in $\frac{6}{8}$ time respond well enough to the interpretation we have described for fast beating, but if we try to "beat quarter notes" (which would mean playing as if the time signature were $\frac{3}{4}$), the accents do not seem to fall in the proper place. Similarly, with anything written in $\frac{3}{4}$ time, it is difficult to "beat half notes". *Whenever the numerator of a time signature is divisible by three, it is usually written in such a way that main stresses fall consistently on every third division:*

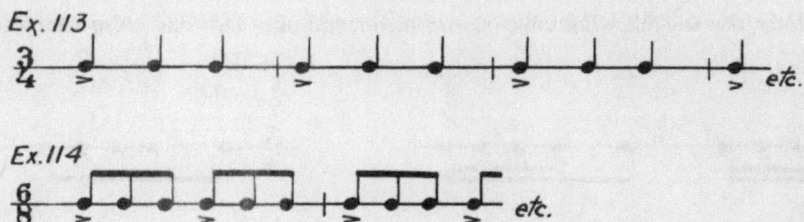

To perform 6/8 time with a slower foot beat, we count, not quarters, but *dotted* quarters ($\frac{6}{8} = \frac{2}{\text{♩.}}$):

which should be thought of as:

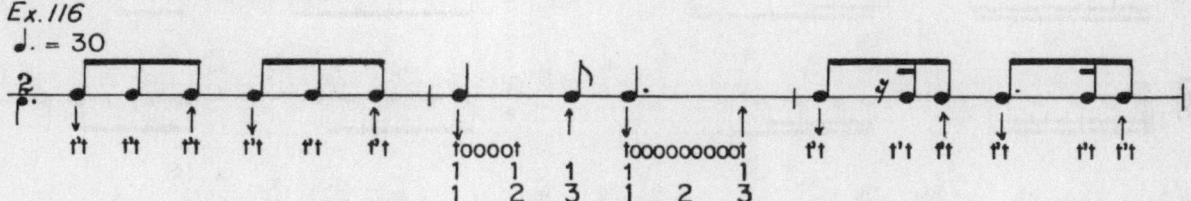

Similarly, with $\frac{3}{4}$ ♩=90 when thought of as $\overset{1}{\text{♩.}}$:

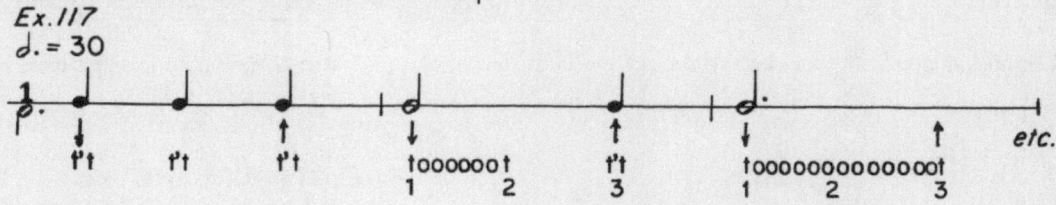

Examples of time signatures frequently done in this way are: $\frac{12}{8}$ $\frac{6}{4}$ $\frac{3}{8}$ $\frac{9}{8}$ *etc.*

When $\frac{4}{4}$ ♩=90 is done like $\frac{2}{2}$ ♩=45, or $\frac{6}{8}$ ♪=90 like $\overset{2}{\text{♩.}}$ ♩.=30, **ties** should be treated **accordingly**:

Ex.118

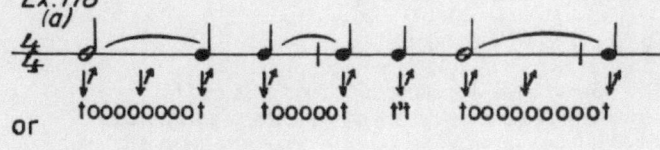

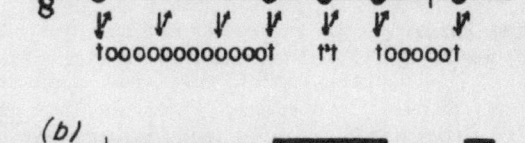

or

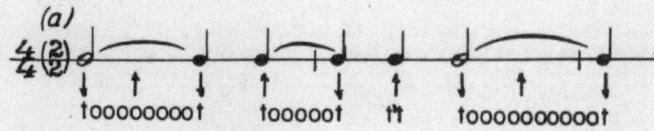

In "fast" $\frac{6}{8}$ time, or other similar "triple-time rhythms", take note of the proper treatment of short note values:

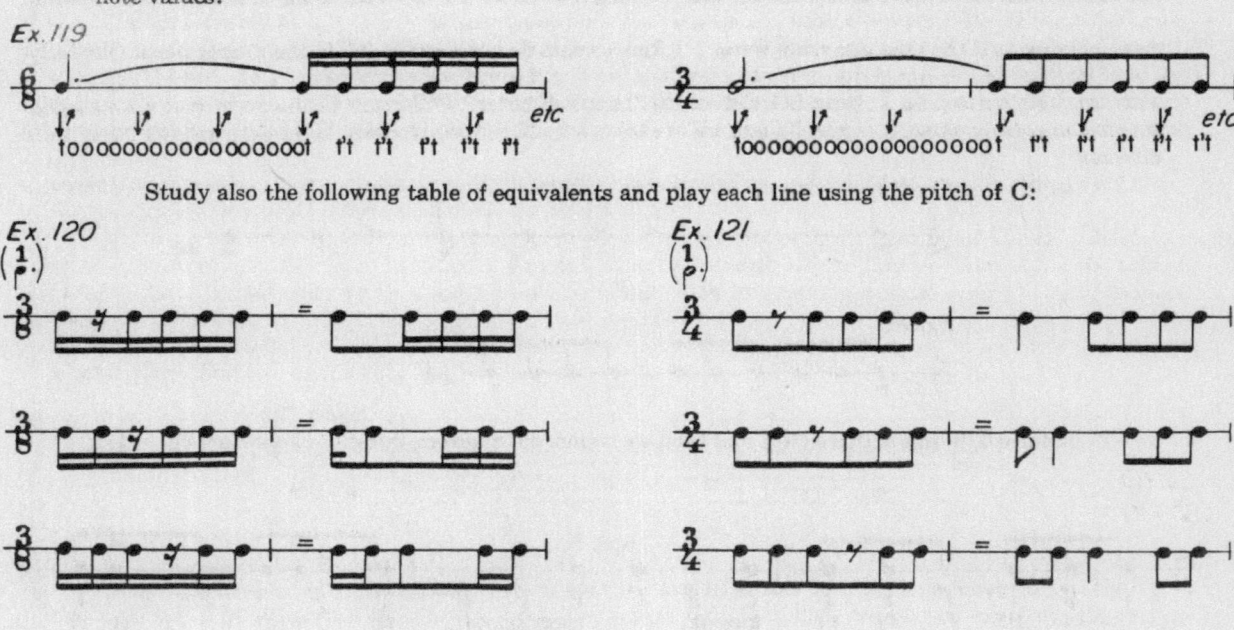

Study also the following table of equivalents and play each line using the pitch of C:

Lesson XIII

THREE HIGH NOTES:

The time has come to study the higher fingerings. The first note to learn is the highest on the instrument:

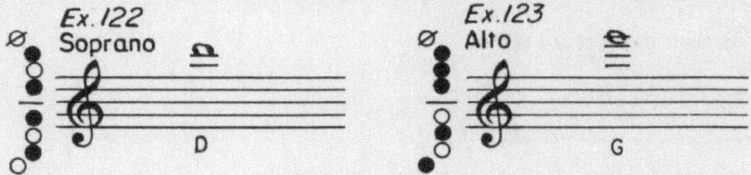

Be sure to tongue clearly and distinctly. We play this note first because it is easier to get than the other two we will cover in this lesson. Here are the other two:

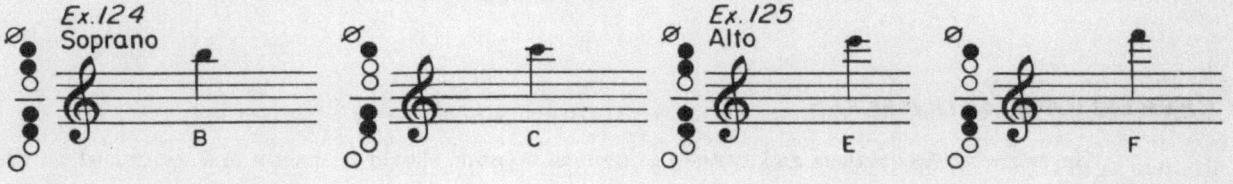

Play the sequence:

Your knowledge of fingerings is now complete, except for one more note which you will learn in Lesson XIV.

RHYTHM: *Some Further Observations*

In Lesson XI, we spoke of "triplets" occurring in music with "duple" time signatures. A triplet may occupy a whole beat:

When this occurs in music, it is necessary to keep the down-motions of the foot equally spaced while modifying the timing of the up-motions to correspond with the number of "notes-per-beat". Try playing the following:

Another peculiarity of rhythm which we must discuss is a holdover from an older system of notation now forgotten except for two symbols. They are used as time signatures, and are explained thus:

$\mathbf{c} = \frac{4}{4}$ (sometimes called *common time*)

$\mathbf{\phi} = \frac{2}{2}$ (sometimes called *alla breve* or *cut time*)

Since, as we learned in the last lesson, $\frac{4}{4}$ and $\frac{2}{2}$ themselves may or may not mean much, it follows that c and ¢ cannot mean much either.

REPETITIONS AND PAUSES

The following designations and symbols in musical notation should be known and recognized by the student:

⌢ or "fermata" (slang term: "Bird's Eye"): When placed over a note, the note should be held beyond its natural duration. When placed over a bar or double bar, the sign may indicate a small interval of silence or, again, it may show the end of a composition.

"Da Capo" or "D. C.": This is placed at the end of a piece of music to indicate to the musician that the first portion is to be played over again as an ending (or conclusion), the ending being marked by the word

"Fine", or the sign ⌢ .

"Dal Segno" or "D. S." (slang term: "Dollar Sign"): This is used instead of Da Capo when the repetition is not from the beginning, but from a point indicated by the sign picture 𝄋 .

"Fine": This word signifies the end of a composition or movement and is generally placed above the staff at the point where the movement ceases after a D. C. or D. S. repetition.

|1.First Ending :|| 2.Second Ending || : When written in a repeated section of music, the first ending is played, after which the strain is immediately repeated. The first ending is then *skipped* on the repetition and the second ending is played instead.

Lesson XIV

LEARNING THE LAST NOTE: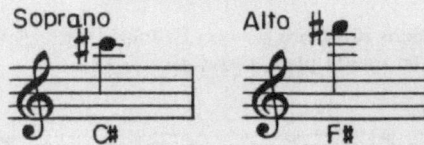

First, let us learn the last fingering, which will bring your knowledge of fingerings to completion:

THE SLUR: ⌒ or ‿

We deal next with an exceedingly important musical device called the *slur*. It looks just like the *tie*, with which we have been dealing since Lesson II. The difference lies in that *it connects individual notes of different pitch*. Another peculiarity is that it may extend over any number of different notes. In all cases, the execution of a slur is identical to that of a tie. As examples:

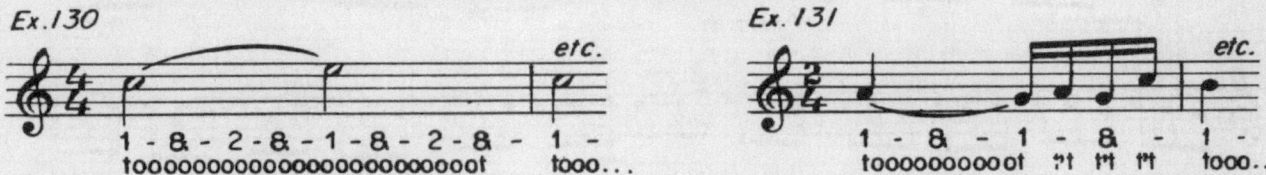

In the first example, the flow of breath (and therefore the sound) is continuous from the beginning of the first ♩ to the end of the second ♩ (which terminates on the "and" of 2). *Simultaneously* with the impact of "1" at the beginning of the second ♩, the fingerings are changed, according to the requirements of the notation, but with no interruption in the stream of air.

It is obviously very important that the fingers involved move instantaneously to the new fingering. Failure to do this results in what we have christened as "bloops" — caused by the tardy arrival of some of the fingers in place.

In the second example, the note on which the slur terminates is less than a beat in length, and that note should therefore be indefinitely short. We show the tongue as *returning* to the roof of the mouth *exactly at the beginning* of the sixteenth note G. This needs some qualification. If the tongue actually operated simultaneously with the fingers, no G would actually sound. It would be cut off before it could start. In actual practice the air will continue to flow for an instant after the fingerings have changed, so that the G actually will sound for a brief instant. That brief instant will be found to be identical with the length of time the other sixteenth notes in the group will sound. All four sixteenth notes, therefore, will be "indefinitely short", but the first of the four will begin not with a motion of the tongue but rather with a motion of the fingers. This will be true of all short-value notes. The following musical selections contain a number of slurs so placed as to give you experience in their correct execution.

MUSICAL SELECTIONS

The first three selections are from Joseph Sellner's "180 Studies..." (*Theoretische-Praktische Oboenschule*). For these, all instruments play in unison.

The following music is taken from the author's recordings with The Telemann Society on Vox, Amphion and other labels:

Les Bouffons

Arbeau-Schulze

Vox Turnabout / TV 340085
Amphion / CL 2143

Mayden Lane
(*English Country Dance*)

(Realization, Schulze)

Vox / STDL 500.470
Amphion / CL 2137

    As soon as you feel you know your size recorder thoroughly, go back through the instruction book and learn another size. This should take about three to four weeks.

    The alto is the "concert" instrument of the recorder family. Beautiful solo and ensemble compositions were written for it by the great masters of the Baroque — Telemann, Handel, Bach, and Mattheson. Because of this, the student should master the alto eventually (no matter what size on which he may have begun) in order to avail himself of this fine literature.

    Be sure to play as much literature as you can. This will help to increase your technical facility. Also, get as much experience as you can playing in groups. Good luck!

A SUMMARY OF ALL RECORDER FINGERINGS

For Soprano and Tenor Recorder

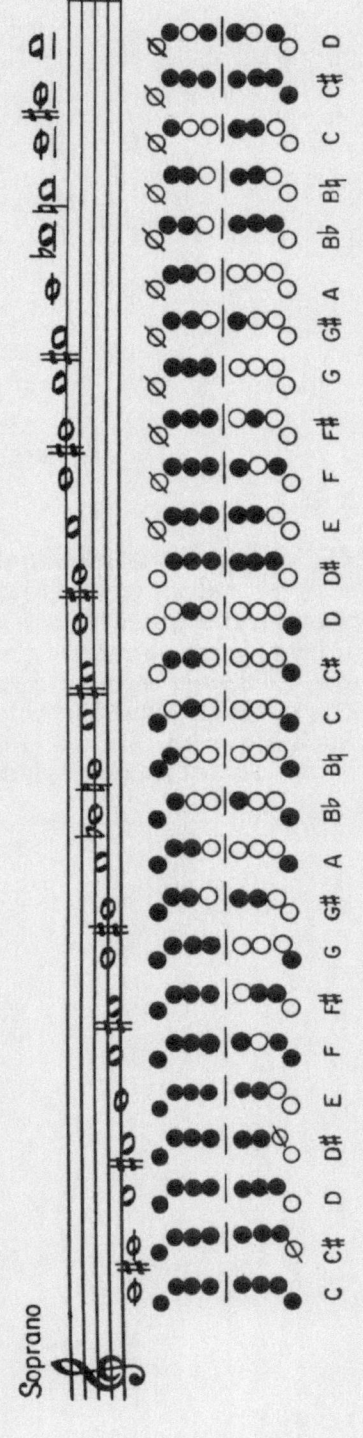

For Alto Recorder

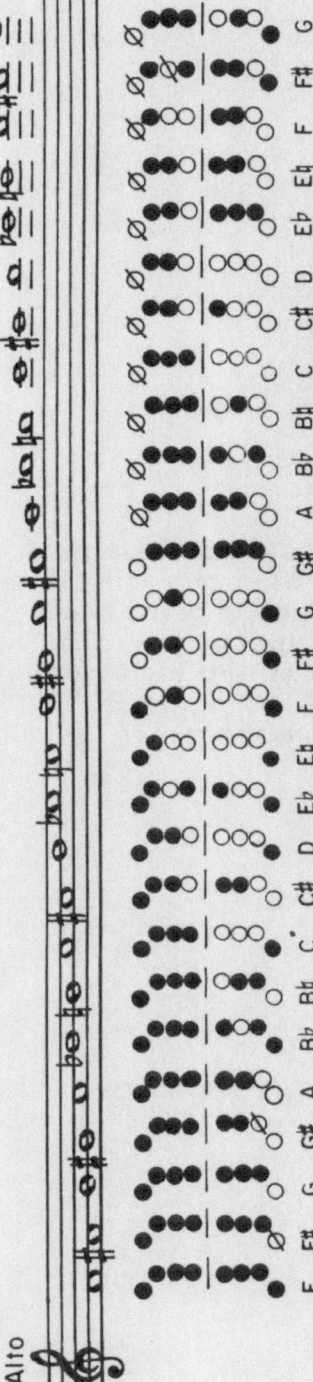

The American Conservatory Press is an outreach activity of the American Conservatory of Music in Belize and Metropolitan Chicago. In order to preserve the proper relationship between academic subjects and comprehensive musical training, the Conservatory has remained entirely independent, and is not affiliated with any college or university. In continuous operation since the year 1886, the Conservatory grants the degrees of Bachelor of Music, Master of Music, and Doctor of Musical Arts. The Conservatory, in addition, grants degrees in Theology, Elocution, and Ecclesiastical Law. The Conservatory has as its sole purpose the preparation of its students for exemplary performance in the art of music and theology in harmony with the objectives and mission of the Eastern Orthodox Church.

The American Conservatory Press
Publication No. 7131. Printed and bound in U.S.A.

www.ingramcontent.com/pod-product-compliance
Lightning Source LLC
Chambersburg PA
CBHW041204020526
44117CB00041B/26